Best-Loved Christmas Carols

Best-Loved Christmas Carols

The Stories Behind Twenty-five Yuletide Favorites

Ronald M. Clancy

Facing page: The Adoration
of the Shepherds
*Giovanni Benedetto Castiglione
(c.1609–1665),
The Louvre, Paris*

Sterling Publishing Co., Inc.
New York

Permission for use of English translation of "O Tannenbaum," p. 70, courtesy of the owners
of The International Book of Carols, Walter Ehret and George K. Evans.

Designed by Adrianne Onderdonk Dudden

2 4 6 8 10 9 7 5 3

Published by Sterling Publishing Co., Inc.
387 Park Avenue South, New York, NY 10016
© 2006 by Christmas Classics, Ltd.
Distributed in Canada by Sterling Publishing
c/o Canadian Manda Group, 165 Dufferin Street,
Toronto, Ontario, Canada M6K 3H6

Printed in China
Sterling ISBN-13: 978-1-4027-4187-6
         ISBN-10: 1-4027-4187-1

For information about custom editions, special sales, premium
and corporate purchases, please contact Sterling Special Sales
Department at 800-805-5489 or specialsales@sterlingpub.com.

Contents

Every effort has been made to identify the sources of pictures. In the event we have not acknowledged any party or organization whose reproduction has not been credited, we offer our sincerest apology. Our gratitude is extended to the curators and staff of the following institutions, museums, collections, and photo agencies for the courtesy of making their images available.

Giovanni Benedetto Castiglione (c.1609–1665), Italian (Mantua), *The Adoration of the Shepherds*, Scala/Art Resource, New York.   *Front cover and 2*

Federigo Barocci (1528–1612), Italian (Urbino), *The Annunciation*, Scala/Art Resource, New York.   *14*

Engraving, *Wassail*, Brothers Dalziel after a painting by Francis Arthur Fraser (c.1835–1900), English, from *Christmas Carols New and Old*, 1871. Courtesy of Antony Miall, London.   *16*

Sandro Botticelli (1445–1510), Italian (Florentine), *The Mystic Nativity*, The National Gallery Picture Library, London.   *18*

Giotto (c.1267–1337), Italian (Florentine), *Christmas in Greccio* (fresco from *Scenes from Legend of St. Francis* at Arena Chapel), Fratelli Alinari, Florence.   *21*

Denys Van Alsloot (c.1570–1628), Flemish, *Procession of the Forty-Eight Guilds and Corporations*, Musees royaux des Beaux-Arts de Belgique (Koninklijke Musea voor Schone Kunsten van Belgie), Brussels.   *22, 23*

Rose Window, Cathedral of Notre-Dame de Paris, North Transept, 13th-century stained glass, Art Resource, New York.   *25*

Lucas Cranach the Elder (1472–1553), German, *Portrait of Martin Luther*, Scala/Art Resource, New York.   *27*

George H. Boughton (1833–1905), American, *Pilgrims Going to Church*, Collection of The New York Historical Society.   *29*

Moravian engraving, *Children's Love Feast*, 1757, "Collection of Old Salem."   *30*

Thomas Webster (1806–1886), English, *A Village Choir*, 1847, Victoria & Albert Museum Picture Library.   *31*

The Illustrated London News, *Christmas Tree at Windsor Castle*, 1848, The Illustrated London News Picture Library.   *32*

George Henry Durrie (1820–1863), American, *Going to Church*, 1853, The White House Collection, copyright White House Historical Society.   *34*

Left panel of *The Wilton Diptych*, c.1395, French School, The National Gallery Picture Library, London.   *38*

Edward Burne-Jones (1833–1921), English, *Angeli Laudantes,* c.1887, design for Salisbury Cathedral, Fitzwilliam Museum, University of Cambridge.   *41*

Engraving by James Bannister (1821–1901) after a painting by Karl A. Schwerdgeburth (1785–1878), German, *Martin Luther and His Family at Wittenberg, Christmas Eve, 1536,* Evangelical Lutheran Church in America.   *43*

James Tissot (1836–1902), French, *The Nativity of Our Lord and Saviour Jesus Christ,* Brooklyn Museum, New York.   *45*

John Callcott Horsley (1817–1903), *Decorating with Holly,* Chris Beetles Ltd., London, UK/The Bridgeman Art Library.   *46*

Berthold Furtmeyr (c.1470–1501), German, *The Tree of Jesse,* miniature illumination from *The Salzburg Missal,* Bayerische Staatsbibliothek, Munich.   *48*

Engraving by R. Brandard (1805–1862) after a painting by Henry Warren (1794–1879), English, *The Star in the East,* Mary Evans Picture Library.   *51*

Rosina Emmett Sherwood (1854–1898), American, *Christmas Music,* 1st prize winner of 1880 Louis Prang Co. Christmas card competition, Boston Public Library Print Department.   *52*

John Leech (1817–1864), English, watercolor, *"Scrooge's Third Visitor,"* from *A Christmas Carol* by Charles Dickens. London: Chapman & Hall, 1843. First Edition, opposite page 78. The Pierpont Morgan Library/Art Resource, New York.   *53*

Francesco de Zurbaran (1598–1664), Spanish, *Blessed Henry Suso,* Museo Provincal de Bellas Artes, Seville.   *55*

Engraving, *Good King Wenceslas,* Brothers Dalziel after a painting by Francis Arthur Fraser (c.1835–1900), English, from *Christmas Carols New and Old,* 1871. Courtesy of Antony Miall, London.   *57*

Gutenberg, Johannes, *Biblia Latina,* Mainz: Johann Gutenberg & Johann Fust, c. 1455, Volume II, f.131v–132. PML 818 ch1 ffl. The Pierpont Morgan Library/Art Resource, New York.   *58*

Caravaggio (1573–1610), Italian (Milanese), *The Young Bacchus,* Scala/Art Resource, New York.   *61*

Victorian book illustration, Anonymous, *Carrying Home the Christmas Holly,* Private Collection/The Bridgeman Art Library.   *62*

American Christmas card, *Glad Tidings,* c. 1880–1885, National Museum of American History (Smithsonian Institution).   *64*

Dora Wheeler (1858–1940), American, *Shout with Joy Ye Mortals Pray,* 2nd place prize winner of 1882 Louis Prang Co. Christmas card competition, National Museum of American History (Smithsonian Institution).   *65*

Pol, Jean, and Herman de Limbourg (active 1400–1416), *Annunciation to the Shepherds,* from *Les Belles Heures de Jean Duc de Berry,* fifteenth-century manuscript illumination. © Photograph, The Metropolitan Museum of Art, The Cloisters Collection, 1954 (54.1.1).   *67*

David Roberts (1796–1864), Scottish, *Church of the Nativity,* 1840, Paisley Museum & Art Galleries, Renfrewshire Council, Paisley, Scotland.   *69*

Aquarell on parchment, *St. Urban's Ritt,* c.1621, Germanisches Nationalmuseum, Nuremberg.   *71*

Fritz von Uhde (1848–1911), German, *Holy Night* (triptych), Sachsische Landesbibliothek-Staats-und Universitatsbibliothek, Dresden; Dezernat Deutsche Fotothek.   *73*

Jan Steen (1626–1679), Dutch, *A Twelfth Night Feast,* 1951 Purchase Fund, courtesy of Museum of Fine Arts, Boston. Reproduced with permission. © Museum of Fine Arts. All Rights reserved.   *75*

Fra Angelico (1387–1455), Italian (Florentine), *The Angels Serve Food to the Monks* (predella from *Coronation of the Virgin* at Convent of San Domenico in Fiesole), Scala/Art Resource, New York.   *79*

Engraving by R. W. Buss (1804–1875), English, *Lady of the Manor Offers Wassail Bowl to Carol Singers,* Mary Evans Picture Library.   *82*

John La Farge (1835–1910), American, *The Three Wise Men,* c.1878, gift of Edward W. Hopper, courtesy Museum of Fine Arts, Boston. Reproduced with permission. © Museum of Fine Arts. All Rights reserved.   *83*

Jacob Jordaens (1593–1678), Flemish, *As the Old Sing, the Young Pipe,* Alte Pinakothek, Munich (Kunstdia-Archiv Artothek).   *87*

Michael Halliday (1822–1869), English, *The Nativity,* stained glass panel from St. Columba Church, Topcliffe, Yorks. Courtesy of Mr. Peter Gibson.   *88*

Rembrandt (1606–1669), Dutch, *The Adoration of the Shepherds,* The National Gallery Print Library, London.   *89*

Peter Paul Rubens (1577–1640), Dutch, *The Adoration of the Magi,* Koninklijke Museum voor Schone Kunsten, Antwerp (Belgie).   *92*

Alexandre-Gabriel Decamps (1803–1860), French, *The Flight into Egypt,* c.1850–1853, Brooklyn Museum, New York.   *98*

Acknowledgments

The inspiration for this collection comes from a number of sources, particularly from close friends and family. A great debt of gratitude is owed to the following people and organizations: Charles Sens and other members of the Library of Congress Music Division; current and former members of Free Library of Philadelphia Music Department, especially Linda Wood, Maureen Cattie, Paula Mentusky, Martha Minor, Judy Harvey, and Sidney Grolnic; the Van Pelt Library of the University of Pennsylvania, particularly Marjorie Hassen and her staff of the Music Division; the Ryan Library staff of St. Charles Seminary, Overbrook, Philadelphia, PA, including Noel McFarren, and Prof. Gerald Malsbary of the Latin Department; the Lutheran Seminary of Philadelphia; Don Ripplinger, former Associate Director of the Mormon Tabernacle Choir, Salt Lake City, and members of his staff; George K. Evans of North Hollywood, CA; Kelly Adams of Beach Park, Illinois; Anthony Clancy of Philadelphia, PA; Michael Wozniak of Savannah, GA; Bill Shisler of ColorComp, Inc. of Pennsauken, NJ; Terry Hogan of Damascus, MD; Mike Maurizi of Bethesda, MD, and his supportive wife Susan, a superb editor who made a considerable contribution to this effort; and Prof. William Studwell, a rich resource and well known authority on Christmas carols.

For helping with the difficult task of assembling the representative images, we are ever in the debt of Adrianne Onderdonk Dudden, a book designer of infinite grace and an eye for what is truly beautiful, and whose design effort was greatly helped by music engravers, Dan Fuqua of Lebanon, NH, and Len and Debbi Oranzi of Wallingford, PA. Aiding in this effort were a host of dedicated librarians, including the late Marietta Boyer of the Pennsylvania Academy of Fine Arts, Philadelphia; members of the University of Pennsylvania Fine Arts Library; Mary Jane Dillon and other staff members of Cape May County Library, Cape May Courthouse, NJ; and staff personnel of the National Museum of American History Prints Department (Smithsonian Institution).

A true professional, one who provided continued encouragement to the concept that information, art, and audio music can be welded effectively as a single package, and who believed in the project years before anyone else did, was John Penn of SONY Music Special Products. Special mention also goes to Joel Adams of Devon Consulting of Wayne, PA, whose friendship exceeded all bounds by allowing use of his company's facility and computer equipment, and to his staff members, past and present, including Santi and Ramana Kanumalla, Dennis Pazicni, Sue Bodalski, Marsha Johnson, Lori Martin, and Amy Bennett.

For their faithful and moral support and for going with me where others had feared to tread, Bob and Mary Ann Scott of Media, PA, are owed much more than they realize. But the greatest debt of gratitude is owed to my wife, Renate, whose unstinting support and patience proved to be tremendous assets during the various stages of the project.

To varying degrees, these individuals and organizations confirmed the value of team effort, professionalism, and attention to detail. Coupled with the contributions of authors of source material, whose works encouraged study and notation, the process of gathering information was thus made fruitful, further earmarking this volume as a truly collaborative effort.

R.M.C.

12 ∞

Best-Loved Christmas Carols

Introduction

Best-Loved Christmas Carols is derived from a larger Christmas music product titled *THE MILLENNIA COLLECTION: Glorious Christmas Music, Songs, and Carols,* a deluxe international collection of 170 titles. The latter was born from the simple curiosity of wanting to know more about the origins and development of Christmas music. There were always intriguing questions. When did Christmas music begin? What did it sound like in the early centuries, or in the thirteenth, or fifteenth, or seventeenth centuries? Many books have been published about Christmas music, predominantly carol collections, but there has been no definitive work tracing the evolution of Christmas music from the early years of Christianity to the modern era.

Much ground was covered to answer these questions in *THE MILLENNIA COLLECTION,* and perhaps the reader might want to seek similar discovery there about the quite fascinating history of Christmas music. One will learn there is considerably more substance to the body of Christmas music than the limited number of traditional religious and secular standards that we are accustomed to hearing repeatedly each holiday season during the course of Christmas shopping, riding in our cars, or just plain relaxing at home. Some of the very best Christmas music actually is performed at various churches or concert halls during Advent, or Christmastide, as part of musical programs staged by professional or amateur groups.

When my friends suggested I pursue the idea of writing about the topic of Christmas music, I took their suggestion with a little trepidation, yet in earnest. Ultimately, after years of trial and effort, *THE MILLENNIA COLLECTION* had a life of its own, and from it *Best-Loved Christmas Carols: The Stories behind Twenty-five Yuletide Favorites* evolved.

Because Christmas music is primarily distinguished by the popularity of its carols, this volume about our favorite carols was designated as a good starting point to begin the exploration of this well-loved, but little-understood, topic. Although there has been quite a number of publications about Christmas carols over the years, many of them, even those of quality and reputation, have not reached a mass audience. One explanation for this phenomenon is that carol publications by their very nature are seasonal, and thus book store owners, particularly in today's highly competitive book trade, believe they do not merit long shelf life. Yet, at the same time, in another part of the marketing world, millions of copies of carols and holiday songs are sold each Christmas season.

Bearing this dichotomy in mind, *Best-Loved Christmas Carols* was created, and during the course of its evolution, I tried to keep to the following objectives:

1— to compile a reasonably comprehensive international collection of Christmas music, songs, and carols, both religious and secular, with special attention to English language or American contributions;

Wassail
Engraving from 1871 English Carol Book

2— to include interesting background information, whenever possible, about each of the carols;

3— to introduce a concise and informative historical perspective about Christmas carols, weaving in information about Christmas traditions and customs wherever possible, thus allowing the reader to understand the cultural context and how they might have sounded at given moments from the fourteenth to the nineteenth century;

4— to adorn the book with beautiful illustrations and art, many of them paintings from some of the great museums of the world, including scenes associated with the Nativity, such as the adoration of the shepherds, the visit of the Magi, as well as festive holiday activities. As much as possible, these images would reflect the country and the period in which a carol was composed; for example, a sixteenth-century German carol would be illustrated by the work of a German artist from the same era, or a nineteenth-century American Christmas greeting card, or painting, would accompany the creation of a nineteenth-century American composer.

5— to provide an exquisite audio collection, which includes the magnificent sounds of such musical stalwarts as the Mormon Tabernacle Choir, the Vienna Boys Choir, the Royal Philharmonic Chorus, and others, with instrumental accompaniment by some of the world's preeminent orchestras, among them the London Symphony and the New York Philharmonic.

The seed of inspiration for *THE MILLENNIA COLLECTION* and its various volumes was probably sown on an early Christmas when I was but one of six hundred boys at St. John's Orphanage in Philadelphia. To this day I have never forgotten the feeling of awe and wonderment I had as a first grader during my first Midnight Mass. The carols that were sung so beautifully by a choir of nuns on that memorable occasion kindled a love that has remained with me throughout the years.

This volume is the legacy I hope to leave to lovers of Christmas carols around the world. Perhaps it may be shared by young children with their doting parents or grandparents, or by mothers and daughters reading to each other, or by a close friend stopping by for a holiday visit. *Best-Loved Christmas Carols* may even cause a harried mother or father lying comfortably in bed after a long day to pause long enough to take comfort in the soothing sounds of Christmas carols. It might serve as a trusty companion book for carolers on their seasonal rounds, or for spiritually or introspectively inclined persons attending a church-sponsored Christmas music program.

If any such ends should be accomplished, then immeasurable satisfaction will have been earned from an untiring effort to contribute something fresh and unique to the rich carol heritage of Christmas. In brief, *Best-Loved Christmas Carols,* was conceived and carried out in the spirit of that wonderful season.

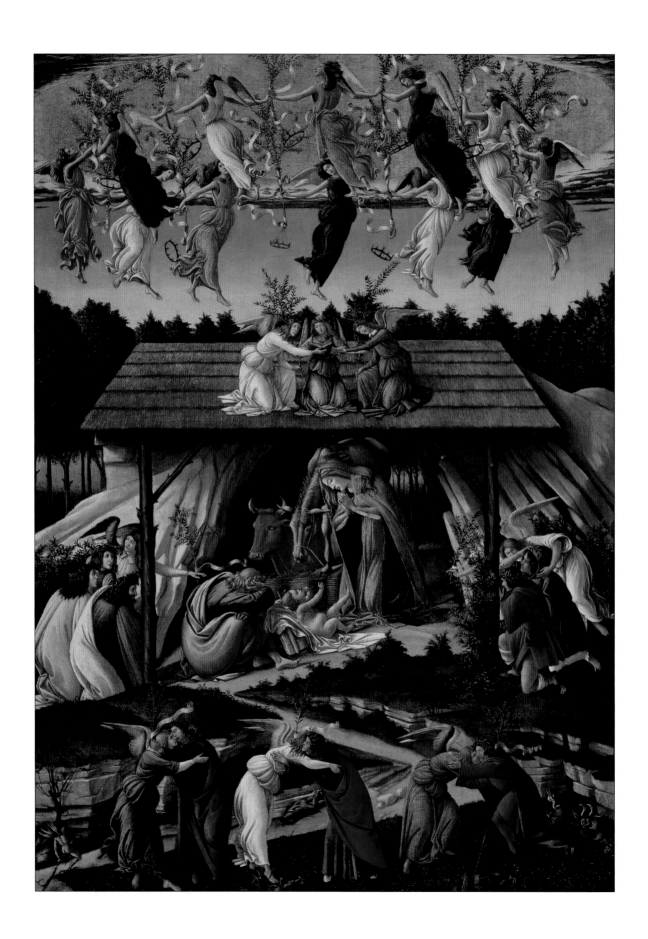

Best-Loved Christmas Carols is a labor of love that was pursued to provide consumers of Christmas audio music, many of them repeat customers, a packaging alternative that not only satisfies their annual needs, but also appeals to their aesthetic inclinations for information and color.

This volume about our favorite Christmas carols offers readers three special elements not normally found in other Christmas music products: 1) well-researched information, 2) wonderful illustrations, and 3) beautiful music. Containing twenty-five of our most familiar carols, primarily from the United Kingdom and the United States, *Best-Loved Christmas Carols* adds carol gems from Germany, France, and Austria to the mix.

To familiarize the reader with how our favorite carols have achieved their time-honored status, the ensuing historical perspective traces the evolution of carols from the fourteenth to the nineteenth century.

The Origin of Carols The first carol, according to legend, was sung by angels appearing to the shepherds of Bethlehem and declaring the birth of Christ and "peace to men of good will" (*Luke 2: 14*). Derived from the French word *carole*, originally meaning a round dance and, in later years, a joyful religious song, the carol is the musical form by which Christmas is best known. The best modern definition of *carol* is probably that of Percy Dearmer (1867–1936), co-author of *The Oxford Book of Carols*, a compilation published in 1928. He described the carol as a song with a religious impulse that is simple, popular, and modern. A carol is folklike in character. It is simple, has little pretense to it, has plain lyrics, and is a seasonal song. Today most people think of carols as strictly Christmas songs, and it is estimated that four to five thousand carols exist, most of them in the realm of the obscure.

In fact, carols originally came from secular and pagan sources. The Greeks sang them in their plays, and the Romans used them during *Saturnalia*, one of their major festivals celebrating the Winter Solstice. They were quite popular and were sung for weddings, birthdays, and other festivities. Later, from the early fourteenth century until the outset of the Reformation, the carol was more aptly defined as a poem suitable for singing, made up of uniform stanzas, and provided with a burden, or an external refrain, repeated after each stanza. Very few vernacular carols were known prior to the fourteenth century due to several reasons: church interference in people's everyday affairs, the predominance of Latin usage, and obscurity.

The fourteenth century witnessed a time of real troubles for the Christian Church. Because of various abuses, the failure to observe religious vows, and the overt worldliness of the clergy, the Church could no longer count on total alle-

Facing page:
The Mystic Nativity
Sandro Botticelli (1445–1510)
The National Gallery, London

giance from its members. In the sphere of music this disengagement contributed to the composition of more secular music, the inspiration for which was found in the nonliturgical world. Secular music even invaded the ecclesiastical sphere, causing bitter complaints from members of the clergy, and Gregorian chant, the preferred music of the Christian Church, began to be eclipsed by the new music.

One might note that for centuries music was given its greatest impetus by the Christian Church. From the dawn of the Church until the late Medieval Era, the history of music in the Western World was related to the liturgy. Music was made to become the servant of the Christian faith, and there is little evidence of the existence of nonliturgical or folk music before the twelfth century, save for precious few extant examples of notated secular music, a point of fact not disputed by historians.

Music was just another area where the Church intruded upon the everyday affairs of its members. Resentment against this intrusion gave rise to the development of the democratic spirit. One way for people to register their displeasure was to write songs, many of them secular in nature, about love, drinking, parodies of church liturgical texts contorted to secular interpretations, the Crusades, and other subjects. By the fourteenth century, songs with vernacular lyrics, as opposed to Church Latin, began to appear more frequently, further laying the groundwork for the developments of carols. With the dawning of the Renaissance, the rise of secular compositions continued unabated. Some of these compositions included carols. Though many carols were religious in content, they were essentially nonliturgical in nature.

The origin of carols cannot be understood without recognizing their linkage to dancing. Like singing in the early Church, dancing had been frowned upon by Church authorities because they considered it immoral and associated with heathen worship. But long before the birth of Christianity, dancing and singing had existed together with religion. The Romans had religious dances, as did the Druids and other religious priests, and eventually these dances found their way into the Christian Church. Dancing in the church, however, was outlawed after the occurrence of some scandals.

The Council of Toledo in 589 and the Council of Avignon in 1209 separately banned dancing entirely from church worship, but dancing still accompanied the singing of songs and carols outside the church. Dancing while singing carols was even part of the outdoor Nativity worship services led by St. Francis of Assisi, and in later centuries performers danced and sang carols during the mystery plays.

Christmas in Grecchio
(fresco from Scenes from
Legend of St. Francis)
*Giotto (c.1267–1337),
Arena Chapel, Padua*

St. Francis and the Crèche Some historians credit St. Francis of
Assisi (1182–1226) for introducing carols (and dancing) in 1223 at the first manger
scene of record in Grecchio, a small Italian village. The townspeople provided inspiration for St. Francis, who had taught God's love by leading a humble and ex-
emplary life, including respect for creatures around him. St. Francis, in turn, encouraged his friars to build a living monument to the "Babe of Bethlehem." They
all believed Christmas should be celebrated as a natural re-enactment of Christ's
birth, a stark contrast to the rigid ceremonial religious rites performed amid so

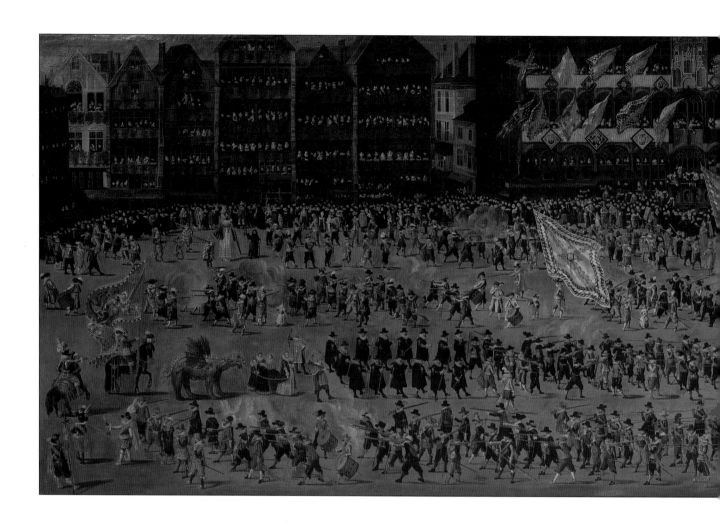

Procession of the
Forty-Eight Guilds and
Corporations
Denys Van Alsloot
(c.1570–1628)
Musees royaux des Beaux-Arts
de Belgique, Brussels

much pretentiousness and ornamentation inside the church. St. Francis requested and was granted special permission from the Pope to conduct Midnight Mass before the manger scene, which was erected in the open air, surrounded by an ox, an ass, sheep, and shepherds, and there he led villagers and friars carrying torch lights in singing carols of the Nativity.

This simple practice of re-enacting the first Christmas slowly spread throughout all of Europe and England. The *crêche* (a French term for "manger" or "crib") scene would become the most cherished Christmas motif in France, and other countries of Europe and Western civilization would forever incorporate the manger theme as part of Christmas festivities.

Along with this development, the singing of carols was flourishing. Anonymous singers, whose works constitute much of this collection, made up joyful songs that were part of an oral tradition long before they became part of the written record. During the latter part of the Medieval Period, from 1095 to 1453, most carols were still sung in Latin, although on an ever-decreasing scale, and after the year 1400, use of the vernacular language for carol compositions was more com-

mon. The Medieval Period was also a time when the democratic spirit continued to emerge, further aiding carol development. Carols were a reaction to the overemphasis of religion, and many of their tunes were sung to profane words. Common people everywhere in Europe wanted to loosen the grasp of the Church on their everyday affairs.

One way of expressing this thirst for more freedom was to dance, write, and sing songs in the vernacular tongue, without any of the restraints of Church Latin. The composition of carols gave people a vent for ordinary expression. Although carol verses might sometimes be sung as a modified form of plainchant or plainsong (referring to Gregorian chant, the medieval liturgical music of the Christian Church), the timeless contemplative melodies of the Church were increasingly forsaken, and so began the era of modern music. Briefly stated, the carol was a modern means through which the ordinary man could express his feelings and temper religion's conservatism. As the feudal order continued to collapse in Europe and England during the fifteenth century, this modernization was largely accomplished.

Influence of Guilds and Mystery Plays   Another influence on the music and songs of the Middle Ages was the production of religious plays by guilds. Guilds could be favorably compared to today's large corporations from an organizational perspective, but they were very protective and against free trade. They also helped to finance churches and cathedrals and to prepare and stage the miracle and mystery plays that were exceedingly popular in Europe and England. Each guild took responsibility for a specific religious scene, providing, besides finances, the costumes and music for the production. Guilds were quite numerous: Venice had fifty-eight; Genoa, thirty-three; Florence, twenty-one; Cologne, twenty-six; and Paris, one hundred; and they were well-represented in every important town in England. The guilds' production of religious plays was an impetus for the flowering of carols, particularly in England, although Latin usage would still be prominent in the thirteenth and early fourteenth centuries.

Mystery plays were also an important source of carols. These plays, with their powerful musical and literary material, helped ordinary people, many of whom were illiterate, learn the Biblical stories. The theme of mystery plays was usually the life of Jesus Christ. (Morality plays involved allegorical representations of various virtues and vices. Miracle plays dealt with the saints and their lives.) These plays were performed either on a fixed stage, where people went to see them, or in a procession in which a series of carts passed as a pageant with people looking on, much as floats in a parade today.

The singing of carols became an integral part of the mystery plays. The audience was quite taken by carols because of their immense appeal, and, on occasion, near riots erupted if these popular songs were not sung during a play's performance. In England, especially, the carol was a byproduct of the mystery plays. The earliest surviving carols were often found in manuscripts relating Biblical or legendary stories of the Nativity, the Virgin Mary, and the Crucifixion—the same stories depicted in the mystery plays. But there were also carols composed for the New Year, drinking and carousing, the commemoration of historical events, and other secular occasions.

Carols in England and Europe   Today we know carols as essentially an English phenomenon, although France, Germany, Italy, Spain, and the Czech Republic (Bohemia and Moravia) have made major contributions to carol development on the European continent. Poland, Austria, Sweden, the Netherlands, and Belgium have also added significantly to the repertoire. The contributions of the United States and other countries of the Western Hemisphere were not felt until the seventeenth, eighteenth, and nineteenth centuries.

Rose Window, Cathedral of
Notre-Dame de Paris,
North Transept
(Virgin and Child *in center*)
thirteenth-century stained glass

The theme of the carol was one of love, particularly in respect to the portrayal of a mother's tender instincts for her child. In the early days of the vernacular carol this maternal picture was also symbolized by the rose, which represented perfection and the Virgin Mary. This symbol of the Virgin Mary could be found in the "rose windows" of the great cathedrals, such as Notre Dame or Chartres, where it was enshrined as masterpiece creations of the Medieval Era.

About five hundred medieval carol manuscripts have survived in England, some in several versions. More than one hundred carols from the late fifteenth and sixteenth century have musical settings in simple melody or elaborate polyphonic settings. The English medieval carol, however, has no connection to the French *noël*, despite the frequent reference to the word "nowell" as an exclamation of joy in a carol. (The subject of English medieval carols could be anything. The French noël, however, was strictly dedicated to Christmas carols.) The word "nowell" was used by Geoffrey Chaucer (c.1340–1400) in his late writings.

The development of carols coincided with that of folk songs and polyphonic music, although the medieval carol settings (music composed or arranged to fit a text) were not derived from folk songs but from a simpler art form. The royal courts of Europe patronized music and musicians, and rulers sponsored choirs in their favorite churches. These choirs were quite attuned to polyphonic music and carols, as well as to secular and folk songs.

Publication of Carols The popularity of carols reached the point where they began to be printed in small books. The first collection of carols may have been printed by 1521 in England by Wynken de Worde (about whom nothing else is known). Some collections contained not only English carols, but also French *noëls* and German Christmas songs. Perhaps the finest collection of carols on the European continent in the sixteenth century was *Piae Cantiones* (meaning "Sacred Songs"). This 1582 songbook was in use for centuries in the Swedish realm, especially in Finland, which was then under Sweden's rule. It had seventy-four songs, less than half from sources in France, England, Germany, and Bohemia (now the Czech Republic). *Piae Cantiones* was compiled by a Finnish student, Theodoricus Petri Rutha, son of an aristocratic land owner, and contained both church and school songs dating from the period 1350 to 1450, including the carol tunes for "Good King Wenceslas" and "Good Christian Men, Rejoice."

By the early sixteenth century the carol had become a more refined form of composition. The richness and color of the Renaissance, plus the increasing secularity that characterized the literature and art of the age, had its influence on song and carol compositions. The poetic texture of carols was still apparent, but the scope of the carol had narrowed to the Advent and Christmas stories. In France the carol, or *noël*, came into greater vogue by the late fifteenth century and was composed specifically for the Christmas season. The first *noëls* supposedly came from songs of troubadours and from songs about St. Francis and his manger scene.

In England, where the carol was composed for any season and might be secular or sacred, the emphasis was moving more toward Christmas themes. The carols "God Rest Ye Merry, Gentlemen" and "The First Nowell" were most likely composed in sixteenth-century England, and from Germany would come the popular "O Tannenbaum." The carol had become popular music, achieving a lofty status during that era, but it would be short-lived in its existing form.

By the sixteenth century the development of music no longer relied on the Church for its greatest support, especially since music was used to challenge Church repression. The influence of the Church, moreover, had continued to wane seriously with respect to matters of the soul, not to mention songs and music. With the ushering in of the Age of Reformation, a whole new dynamic was

Portrait of Martin Luther
Lucas Cranach the Elder
(1472–1553),
Galleria degli Uffizi, Florence

reshaping the religious landscape of Christian Europe. The history of this change would also affect Christmas and its music.

The Reformation   Martin Luther (1483–1546), a German monk and leader of the Reformation, was a lover of German music and folk songs, which may have been the finest in Europe. He felt that the Church liturgy was too aristocratic, having become snobbish over the years and too detached from the common people. This detachment was embodied in the Church's practice of keeping the priest and the all-male choir who sang the Mass separated from the worshippers.

Luther sought reforms in music, as he sought change in theology, ethics, ritual, and art. He loved polyphony and wanted music that would move people by fusing faith and song. Luther encouraged a greater participation by the congregation in singing, and he simplified the music from choir plainsong to easy harmony, thus reducing the role and influence of the Mass. In the sixteenth and seventeenth centuries the Reformation extended the range of choral music beyond the liturgy, and the informal group singing of songs was highly encouraged, leading to a greater familiarity with Christmas hymns.

The founders of some Protestant sects did not like the idea of music being played at all in the church, however, and put limits on such activities. Their restrictions also led to a sharp reduction of boisterous observances of Christmas, although they welcomed joyful hymns as long as they adhered to scriptural meaning.

In England, the extremes of the Reformation were being carried out by the Puritans, who reverted to the strictness of the Dark Ages. The Puritans strongly disliked music in churches and abolished it because they considered music an obstacle separating God from the worshipper. They advocated "blue" Sundays and detested how Christmas was celebrated with merrymaking, dancing, and singing. They attributed many Christmas customs to pagan origins and demanded that Christmas be made a solemn day of atonement.

In a 1644 decree from the Puritan Parliament, Christmas was declared a fast day, as it fell on the last Wednesday of the month, which at that time was preserved and commemorated as the normal fast day. In 1647 Christmas was abolished entirely. The severity of these restrictions would influence the English people to believe that dancing before the altar was an embarrassment. Even with the onset of the Restoration and the ascension of Charles II to the throne of England in 1660, the Puritans would retain spiritual sway in England and America.

Carols fell into disfavor during the Reformation because of their linkage to Catholic Rome and its "superstitious practices," and because they had lost much of their vitality with the changing of the religious temper of the sixteenth cen-

Pilgrims Going to Church
George H. Boughton
(1833–1905),
Collection of The New York
Historical Society

tury. In the English-speaking world, the Puritan extremes led to a two-hundred-year hiatus of quality carol composition. The English Reformation, which had begun with the suppression of Christmas rites and celebration and had influenced the further decline of Latin and lullaby carols, witnessed the rise of carefree secular carols, merrymaking, dancing, and drinking, only to have these excesses quickly halted by the strict Puritans. One of the positive aspects of this period was that all of the distress caused by the Puritan regime nurtured a deeper understanding, and a more serious inward turning, of the religious spirit of Christmas.

Carols of the Seventeenth and Eighteenth Centuries In the countryside, the common folk of the seventeenth century kept the spirit of the carol alive, despite the disapproval of the upper classes and the Protestant churches, inside of which the Crucifixion was considered much more important than the Nativity. Such severe religious emphasis also contributed to the decline of the carol.

In America the Puritan restrictions on Christmas affected the colonies of New England. The Pilgrims, who landed at Plymouth Rock in 1620, shunned any observance of Christmas Day and treated it as a normal working day. In 1659, a law passed by the Massachusetts Bay Colony forbade anyone from "observing any such day as Christmas," or that person would be fined five shillings. The law

Children's Love Feast
(*A Christmas Eve feast
of buns and coffee attended by
A pastor, B boys, C girls, and
D & E servers.*)
*Moravian engraving, 1757,
"Collection of Old Salem"*

remained on the books for twenty-two years. Even after Christmas was fully restored in England, its observance was still severely opposed in New England for many years.

In other regions of North America and the colonies, however, Christmas was highly celebrated by pageantry and song. The Dutch in New Amsterdam, the French in Louisiana and Missouri, the Episcopalians in Virginia, and the Moravians in Bethlehem, Pennsylvania, and Winston-Salem, North Carolina, sang carols at Christmas time as they had in their native countries. America's southern colonies celebrated Christmas in aristocratic fashion.

The English form of narrative ballad-like Christmas texts, which had little connection with the medieval carol, was hawked on English streets as broadside ballads cheaply printed and sung to popular tunes of the times. These ballads also appeared in the American colonies during the eighteenth century and could be found along with native folk hymns. Many of these early hymns were crude in form because the colonial composer was less exposed to sophisticated music and less educated, by and large, than the English composer. Like his Old World counterpart, though, his songs of the people were readily understood.

Churchgoers in the American colonies in the late seventeenth to early eighteenth century were likely to sing the hymns of Isaac Watts (1674–1748), the English poet, since they were still closely allied to Puritanism, spurning most carols in favor of hymns. Watts wrote the poem "Joy to the World;" but it would be another 120 years before the American music teacher, Lowell Mason (1792–1872), would compose the music for Watts's lyrics.

During the eighteenth century the carol endured a precarious existence, yet a few important carols were composed. The lyrics of "Hark! The Herald Angels Sing" were penned by Charles Wesley (1707–1788), an English clergyman and co-founder of Methodism. "Adeste Fideles" was composed around 1740 by an English Catholic exiled to Douai, France. However, compared to the beautiful carol gems of the fourteenth- and fifteenth-century England—such as "There is No Rose," "The Boar's Head Carol," and "Lullay My Liking"—the quality of the English carol in the eighteenth century paled.

The quality of carol coming from the European continent was considerably better. The French *noël*, such as "Les Anges dans nos campagnes," demonstrated the typical French flair for grace and charm. German carols manifested the religious and tender impulses of their composers.

A Village Choir, 1847
Thomas Webster (1806–1886),
Victoria & Albert Museum

Nineteenth-Century Carols and Christmas Customs

In churches, Protestants of all denominations dictated exclusive use of the vernacular for all divine services. The Lutherans especially relished the hymns of Martin Luther or the harmonization of German hymns by Bach. In England, Scotland, and the United States, prayers were spoken and hymns sung in the English language. Yet in the great cathedrals and churches of France, Spain, and Italy, and in the rough-hewn churches of Catholic parishes and colonies in the New World, the language of Latin dominated the Mass and other Catholic services. Gregorian chant was still employed, most often accompanied by instrumental music.

The status of the carol, meanwhile, was stagnant in England. The effects of the Puritan era still could be felt by churchgoers in the early nineteenth century. In the countryside, though, common people maintained the oral traditions and kept some of the carols alive and vibrant. In 1822 Davies Gilbert of England compiled a carol collection titled *Some Ancient Christmas Carols* and had it published. The first of several important carol collections that would be published in nineteenth-century England, Gilbert's compilation seemed to address the unfulfilled needs of the public for the resurrection of carols, especially old English folk carols.

Eleven years later another collection of English carols was compiled by William Sandys. The 1833 printing of *Christmas Carols, Ancient and Modern* helped to further revive interest in the English carol. Or was it really the other way around? The people's interest in carols may have spurred the printing of them.

In the successive years of 1839 and 1840, the music for "Joy to the World" and "Hark! The Herald Angels Sing" was composed, although the music for the latter, the work of Felix Mendelssohn (1809–1847), was intended as a musical celebration for the 400th anniversary of the invention of printing by Johann Gutenberg (c.1400–1468). In 1843 an important seasonal literary work by Charles Dickens had a large impact, especially when it was enacted on the theater stage. His classic, *A Christmas Carol*, won over a large audience that enjoyed the singing of carols and other aspects of Christmas celebration. This was the very same year the first Christmas card was created in England.

With the presence of the German Prince Albert, Queen Victoria's consort, at Windsor Castle, German Christmas customs, such as setting up a Christmas tree, became more fashionable in English court life. When a picture of the tree at Windsor Castle was published in an 1848 edition of *The London Illustrated News*, the English populace eagerly emulated their trend-setting monarchs.

Dickens' contemporary in the United States, Washington Irving (1783–1859), loved English customs and traditions. With carol singing and celebrations of Christmas sweeping the English public, Irving, through his writings, encouraged his fellow Americans to partake of similar holiday festivities. This was no simple matter. America had disdained anything associated with the English since the end of the Revolutionary War. As they distanced themselves from English traditions, they were more apt to adopt Christmas customs brought to America by Dutch explorers from much earlier years. Even Washington Irving had prominently mentioned "Sinta Klaes," the venerable Dutch figure of St. Nicholas, six times in his *The Knickerbocker History of New York*.

Irving's endorsement of English Christmas customs, the influence of Prince Albert and Queen Victoria in England and the United States, plus the popularity of *A Christmas Carol* helped to develop the American carol. American song writers soon made significant contributions to the international carol repertoire. In 1849 Edmund H. Sears (1810–1876), a clergyman, wrote the poem "It Came Upon the Midnight Clear." James S. Pierpont (1822–1893) wrote the words and music for "Jingle Bells" in 1857, the first and most famous of American secular carols. In the same year John H. Hopkins (1820–1891) composed "We Three Kings of Orient Are." Another poem made famous as a carol was "O Little Town of Bethlehem," written by the Rev. Phillips Brooks (1835–1893) in 1868 for his Sunday-school children in Philadelphia. These new carols of the mid-nineteenth century helped to end the two-hundred-year drought of quality English-language carols.

Elsewhere in the Christian world, original carols were composed between 1800 and 1850. On a cold Christmas Eve in 1818, a Catholic priest and the church organist of their small village church in Austria had to improvise for music when the church organ broke down. They proceeded to compose a quiet, dignified carol accompanied by guitar. Their effort produced one of the most stirring carols ever written, "Stille Nacht, heilige Nacht" ("Silent Night"). In Catholic France, some Church authorities regarded "Cantique de Noël" ("O Holy Night"), written in 1847, as a distasteful bit of music, and, as usual, the people thought otherwise. They loved it!

Going to Church, *1853*
George Henry Durrie
(1820–1863),
The White House Collection

A movement to sing carols inside Protestant churches emerged in England. English church elders were not enthusiastic about this development. Some of the carols, they felt, were less serious and more festive in nature—certainly not the type to be sung in church. "Good King Wenceslas" and "The Holly and the Ivy" were carols put into this category. From the middle to late nineteenth century, the English people had come to accept the popularity of carols both inside and outside their churches. They enjoyed the continual publication of Christmas carols, eagerly bringing them home to their families and friends. Important carol publications of this period were: 1) *Collection of Ancient Christian Carols* (1860) by Edmund Sedding, a Catholic author, who along with John Mason Neale was part of the Oxford Movement that sought to revive Catholic liturgy; 2) *Songs of the Nativity* (1868) by W. H. Husk; 3) *Christmas Carols New and Old* (1871) by H. R. Bramley and Dr. John Stainer; and 4) the two editions of *Carols for Use in Church* (1875 and 1894) by R. R. Chope.

In the United States, another important carol hymn was published in 1885. "Away in a Manger" was actually an anonymous Christmas composition that for years had been erroneously attributed to Martin Luther, even being titled in his name as "Luther's Cradle Hymn." The rightful composer of the music for this lovely carol was discovered to be James Murray (1841–1905), an American compiler of song books.

When the nineteenth century came to a close, the carol had reclaimed its rightful place in the hearts of English-speaking people everywhere. The shadows from the Puritan clouds had finally receded. The carol was in a robust state of health, and the twentieth century would witness its continued growth.

Success of Carols Continues   The increased popularity of carols continued unabated well into the twentieth century. Newer methods of transmitting music—beginning with the late-nineteenth-century introduction of the phonograph, and in later decades successive technology leaps to radio and television—helped to sustain the ever-increasing demand for Christmas carols and songs. Even popular singers from the United States and Europe, including famous personalities employed by the opera, were recording favorite carols. Their musical efforts were rewarded by an eager audience, and as the century moved along marketers of the genre noticed the trend of ever-increasing sheet music and audio recording sales.

To a large extent, the increase in sales of Christmas music was a direct result of sophisticated marketing techniques used to promote music, especially when popular singers recorded their own Christmas albums. To some degree, these techniques have helped to preserve the legacy of Christmas carols, even if the methods of promoting Christmas music collections have grown static through decades of heavy reliance on familiar marketing formulas.

But the richness of the carol bounty in this volume has less to do with what has transpired in the modern era. Credit goes largely to the carol composers and collectors from the fourteenth to nineteenth centuries, many of them anonymous, who hailed from the countryside of England, Europe, and the United States. It was they who first preserved the contemporary and exciting carol style of music, either through the oral tradition or by publication. The fact that some of them had to overcome periods of religious repression, and the often fickle objections of conservative church elders, only adds more luster to their accomplishments.

As each new Christmas season falls upon us, we might be mindful that our carol heritage was begun and sustained over the centuries by the inspired efforts of intrepid carol composers and collectors. Their contributions were especially significant, and we are forever in their debt. To them we dedicate this volume, *Best-Loved Christmas Carols*.

Best-Loved Christmas Carols

1 ✳ *Adeste Fideles*

English Title—
O Come All Ye Faithful

Recording Artists—
Vienna Boys Choir &
The London Symphony
Orchestra

Words & Music—
John Francis Wade
(1711–1786), English
songwriter and music
teacher

The miniature masterpiece "Adeste Fideles" was composed by John Francis Wade, a Roman Catholic, between 1740 and 1743. The Latin lyrics were first published in 1760 in *Evening Offices of the Church,* and the melody and lyrics were printed together in a London publication, *An Essay on the Church Plain Chant*, in 1782. One of the most popular of those Christmas hymns intended to be sung as part of a church service, it is now sung in both Protestant and Catholic churches throughout the world.

Some authorities erroneously believe the carol was an old Latin piece originally danced and sung around the *crèche*. Other authorities incorrectly attribute it to St. Bonaventura (1221–1274), a Franciscan scholar who was but five years old when the pious founder of his religious order, St. Francis of Assisi, died. In addition, some sources say that the tune was written by John Redding (d.1692), another Englishman, but music research scholars dismiss this claim as inauthentic. Since the end of the eighteenth century, the hymn has been sung at Benediction of the Mass during the Christmas season in England and France.

Wade was a resident at the English College in Douai, France, where he copied, taught, and sold music in addition to providing music lessons for children. In 1852 the Rev. Francis Oakeley (1802–1880), an English clergyman who became a convert to the Roman Catholic Church, published the English lyrics, although he had translated the Latin text eleven years earlier. Oakeley's original text started with a more rigid phrasing, *"Ye faithful, approach ye."*

"Adeste Fideles" has also been referred to as "The Portuguese Hymn," because it was believed for a time to have been first sung by the famous choir of the Portuguese Chapel in London. This would not have been an unlikely scenario, as Wade was known to have corresponded with prominent Catholic musicians of the foreign embassy chapels there, including Thomas Arne (1720–1778), a highly respected English composer. Although an integral part of the modern Christmas music repertoire, the beauty of "Adeste Fideles" is the preservation of its ancient lyrical moorings.

LATIN	ENGLISH
Adeste fideles,	O come, all ye faithful,
Laeti triumphantes;	Joyful and triumphant,
Venite, venite in Bethlehem:	O come ye, O come ye to Bethlehem;
Natum videte	Come and behold Him,
Regem Angelorum:	Born the King of Angels:
REFRAIN:	REFRAIN:
Venite adoremus,	O come, let us adore Him
Venite adoremus,	O come, let us adore Him,
Venite adoremus,	O come, let us adore Him,
Dominum.	Christ, the Lord.

Facing page:
Madonna and Child with
Angels *(left panel of*
The Wilton Diptych)*, c.1395,*
The National Gallery, London

Deum de Deo,
Lumen de Lumine,
Gestant puellae viscera;
Deum verum,
Genitum non factum:
    REFRAIN:

Cantet nunc io
Chorus Angelorum;
Cantet nunc aula celestium,
Gloria
In excelsis Deo:
    REFRAIN:

Ergo qui natus
Die hodierna,
Jesu, tibi sit gloria:
Patris aeterni
Verbum caro factum!
    REFRAIN:

God of God,
Light of Light,
Lo, He abhors not the Virgin's womb.
Very God,
Begotten, not created:
    REFRAIN:

Sing, choirs of Angels,
Sing in exultation,
Sing, all ye citizens of heaven above,
Glory to God
In the highest:
    REFRAIN:

Yea, Lord, we greet Thee,
Born this happy morning.
Jesu, to Thee be glory given;
Word of the Father,
Now in flesh appearing!
    REFRAIN:

Recording Artists—
The Ambrosian Singers;
John McCarthy, conductor;
Leon Goossens, oboe, Marie
Goossens, harp; with organ
and chimes

Words—
James Montgomery
(1771–1854), Scottish
newspaper editor and song-
writer

Music—
Henry Smart (1813–1879),
English composer and
organist

The words for "Angels from the Realms of Glory" first appeared in the Sheffield, Scotland, newspaper the *Iris* on Christmas Eve in 1816. Written by James Montgomery, a journalist and editor of that newspaper for thirty-one years, the lyrics would have come naturally to this devout Christian, who composed hundreds of hymns during his lifetime. Montgomery was quite popular with his readership. In the early days of his newspaper career, he dared to criticize local government authorities, an action that caused his imprisonment on two occasions. He championed a number of unpopular causes, including the abolition of slavery and reform for boy chimney-sweeps. In addition, he was a strong advocate

Angeli Laudantes *(cartoon for Salisbury Cathedral), Edward Burne-Jones (1833–1921), Fitzwilliam Museum, University of Cambridge*

of the Bible Society and overseas missions. Making the most of one prison stay, he wrote a book titled *Prison Amusements,* which served to bring him more admirers, much to the chagrin of the town's political establishment.

At first, the music for "Angels from the Realms of Glory" was the tune written for the eighteenth-century French carol "Les Anges dans nos campagnes" (which also inspired Montgomery's lyrics). This is the tune that was sung almost exclusively in England. However, in the United States another tune called "Regent Square," composed by Henry Smart, would eventually replace the original melody. What makes Henry Smart's contribution to the Christmas repertoire all the more remarkable is that he had gone blind two years before composing the music. Today, only three to four stanzas are usually sung, although the original composition had five stanzas.

Angels from the realms of glory,
Wing your flight o'er all the earth;
Ye, who sang creation's story,
Now proclaim Messiah's birth.
REFRAIN:
Come and worship, come and worship,
Worship Christ the new-born King.

Shepherds in the fields abiding,
Watching o'er your flocks by night,
God with man is now residing;
Yonder shines the infant light.
REFRAIN:

Sages, leave your contemplations,
Brighter visions beam afar;
Seek the great Desire of nations;
Ye have seen His natal star.
REFRAIN:

Saints before the altar bending,
Watching long in hope and fear,
Suddenly the Lord, descending,
In His temple shall appear.
REFRAIN:

Though an infant now we view him,
He shall fill his Father's throne,
Gather all the nations to him;
Every knee shall then bow down.
REFRAIN:

3 ✳ Away in a Manger

Recording Artists—
Royal Philharmonic
Orchestra & Chorus;
Peter Knight, conductor

Words—
Anonymous eighteenth-
to nineteenth-century
American folk

Music—
James Ramsey Murray
(1841–1905), American
composer and music
compiler

A well-known carol hymn of obscure origins, "Away in a Manger" may have been composed by a member of the German Lutheran colony in Pennsylvania during the late nineteenth century. For years, the hymn was thought to have been composed by Martin Luther, the great German religious reformer, and was often referred to as "Luther's Cradle Hymn." However, by the 1940s it was proven conclusively that the music for "Away in a Manger" was actually composed by James Ramsey Murray, the person who had perpetrated the myth of "Luther's Cradle Hymn." Murray, who probably allowed his fanciful imagination to get the better of him, certainly not the first time that someone got heady from the Christmas experience, published his lullaby in an 1887 Cincinnati collection called *Dainty Songs for Lads and Lasses.* Since then, at least forty-one known tunes have been associated with the carol, including those of Jonathan E. Spillman (1812–1896) and William J. Kirkpatrick (1838–1921), whose familiar settings are more likely to be heard in England.

The anonymous words for the first two stanzas appeared several years earlier (1885) in the *Little Children's Book for Schools and Families*, a publication of the Evangelical Lutheran Church in North America. These words may have come from a poem commemorating the 400th anniversary of the birth of Martin Luther. Although many modern hymnals attribute the lyrics of the third stanza to John T. McFarland (1851–1913), a member of the American Lutheran Board of Sunday Schools, it is believed that he had merely made reference to it. The third stanza, which first appeared in an 1892 Louisville, Kentucky, Lutheran Church collection titled *Gabriel's Vineyard Songs*, is probably the contribution of another anonymous author. This lyrical addition strengthens the inherent tenderness of this renowned American carol hymn.

Martin Luther and His Family at Wittenberg, Christmas Eve, 1536, Engraving by John Bannister (1821–1901), Evangelical Lutheran Church in America

Away in a manger, no crib for a bed,
The little Lord Jesus laid down His sweet head.
The stars in the bright sky looked down where He lay,
The little Lord Jesus asleep on the hay.

The cattle are lowing, the Baby awakes,
But little Lord Jesus no crying He makes.
I love Thee, Lord Jesus, look down from the sky,
And stay by my cradle till morning is nigh.

Be near me, Lord Jesus, I ask Thee to stay
Close to me forever and love me I pray.
Bless all the dear children in Thy tender care,
And take us to heaven to live with Thee there.

Other French Title—
Minuit Chrétiens

English Title—
O Holy Night

Recording Artists—
RCA Victor Singers; Richard Westenburg, conductor

Words—
Placide Cappeau
(1808–1877), French poet

Music—
Adolphe Adam
(1803–1856), French composer, pianist, and music teacher

Written in 1847 and first published around 1855, "Cantique de Noël" ("O Holy Night") was originally disliked by French church authorities who criticized the carol for its perceived lack of musical taste. The carol did not sound like typical church music, instead possessing a more emotional and secular feel. This would not be the first time that conservative church officials had objected to something new and different, although their repudiation of the song was more likely due to Placide Cappeau's later renunciation of both Christianity and his 1847 lyrics. French churchgoers, however, had an entirely different reaction to this exotic new carol: it was quite popular with them.

The composer of the music, Adolphe Adam, was better known for his ballets, particularly his well-acclaimed *Giselle*. John Sullivan Dwight (1818–1893), an American clergyman, writer of music, and co-founder of the Harvard Music Society, translated the carol. His English translation is used most frequently today. No matter in which language the carol is sung, the beauty, vibrancy, and unmistakable dramatic phrasing of "Cantique de Noël" adds luster to the ever-growing Christmas repertoire.

FRENCH

Minuit, chrétiens, c'est l'heure solennelle
Où l'Homme Dieu descendit jusqu' a nous.
Pour éffacer la tâche originelle
Et de son Père apaiser le courroux.
Le monde entier tressaille d'espérance
En cette nuit qui lui donne un Sauveur.
Peuple à genoux, attends ta délivrance,
Noël, Noël, voici le Rédempteur!
Noël, Noël, voici le Rédempteur.

De notre foi que la lumière ardente
Nous guide tous au berceau de l'enfant,
Comme autrefois une étoile brillante
Y conduisit les chefs de l'Orient.
Le Roi des rois nait dans une humble crêche;
Puissants du jour, fiers de votre grandeur.
A votre orgueil c'est de l'à qu'un Dieu prêche.
Courbez vos fronts devant le Rédempteur!
Courbez vos fronts devant le Rédempteur!

Le Rédempteur a brisé toute entrave,
La terre est libre et le ciel est ouvert;

Il voit un frère où n'était qu'un esclave;
L'amour unit ceux qu'enchaînait le fer
Qui lui dira notre reconnaissance?
C'est pour nous tous qu'il nait, quil souffre et meurt.
Peuple, debout, chante ta délivrance.
Noël, Noël, chantons le Rédempteur!
Noël, Noël, chantons le Rédempteur!

ENGLISH

The Nativity of Our Lord
and Saviour Jesus Christ,
James Tissot (1836–1902),
Brooklyn Museum

O holy night, the stars are brightly shining;
It is the night of the dear Savior's birth.
Long lay the world in sin and error pining,
Till He appeared and the soul felt its worth.
A thrill of hope, the weary soul rejoices,
For yonder breaks a new and glorious morn.
Fall on your knees, Oh, hear the angel voices!
O night divine, O night, when Christ was born!
O night, O holy night, O night divine.

Led by the light of Faith Serenely beaming,
With glowing hearts by His cradle we stand.
So, led by light of a star sweetly gleaming,
Here came the wise men from Orient land.
The King of Kings lay thus in lowly manger,
In all our trials born to be our friend;
He knows our need, our weakness is no stranger;
Behold your King! Before Him lowly bend!
Behold your King! Before Him lowly bend!

Truly He taught us to love one another,
His law is love, and His gospel is peace;
Chains shall He break, for the slave is our brother,
And His name all oppression shall cease.
Sweet hymns of joy in grateful chorus raise we,
Let all within us praise His holy name;
Christ is the Lord, O praise His name forever!
His pow'r and glory evermore proclaim!
His pow'r and glory evermore proclaim!

5 ✳ *Deck the Halls with Boughs of Holly*

Other Title—
Deck the Halls

Recording Artist—
Norman Luboff Choir

Words & Music—
Anonymous sixteenth-
century Welsh folk

Very little is known about this familiar and popular Welsh carol. The melody can be found in a 1784 song collection titled *Musical and Poetical Relicks of the Welsh Bards*, but it is associated with another Welsh carol known as "Nos Galan" (meaning "New Year's Eve"). Wolfgang Amadeus Mozart (1756–1791), the great Austrian composer, used the melody for one of his compositions, a duet for violin and piano.

Decorating with Holly,
John Callcott Horsley
(1817–1903),
Chris Beetles Ltd., London

The familiar lyrics, whose first known printing was in the 1881 New York publication *The Franklin Square Song Collection,* are sometimes thought to have originated in America perhaps because Washington Irving, a nineteenth-century author and devotee of English traditions and customs, was influential in encouraging carol composing and singing in America. By his time the Puritan influence on Christmas customs had been loosened both in England and the United States.

One of our cheeriest Christmas carols, "Deck the Halls with Boughs of Holly," was sung in the style of madrigals, or simple poetry set to music. Italian and English madrigals of the sixteenth century consisted of twelve lines of poetry sung to music. English madrigals could be more festive and humorous and include nonsensical words, such as "fa la la." The roots of the Italian madrigal came from medieval times.

Deck the halls with boughs of holly,
Fa la la la la la la la la.
'Tis the season to be jolly,
Fa la la la la la la la la.
Don we now our gay apparel,
Fa la la la la la la la la.
Troll the ancient Yuletide carol,
Fa la la la la la la la la.

See the blazing Yule before us,
Fa la la la la la la la la.
Strike the harp and join the chorus,
Fa la la la la la la la la.
Follow me in merry measure,
Fa la la la la la la la la.
While I tell of Yuletide treasure,
Fa la la la la la la la la.

Fast away the old year passes,
Fa la la la la la la la la.
Hail the new, ye lads and lasses,
Fa la la la la la la la la.
Sing we joyous songs together,
Fa la la la la la la la la.
Heedless of the wind and weather,
Fa la la la la la la la la!

6 ❋ *Es ist ein' Ros' entsprungen*

English Title—
Lo, How a Rose E'er
Blooming

Recording Artist—
The DePaur Chorus;
Leonard DePaur, conductor

Words & Music—
Anonymous fifteenth-
century German folk

The original version of the exquisite "Es ist ein' Ros' entsprungen" may have come from the German Rhineland, with no less than twenty-two stanzas. Later reduced to a mere sixteen-stanza piece, this classic is now normally sung in one, two, or three stanzas. The carol has had several English translations, including the first two stanzas here by the noted American music scholar, Theodore Baker (1851–1934). The translation for the third stanza is credited to Harriet R. K. Spaeth (1845–1925). There are a number of other titles and interesting versions, including an 1896 chorale prelude by Johannes Brahms (1833–1897).

The music was first published in the Catholic hymnal *Geistliche Kirchengesang* from Cologne around 1599 or 1600, and the text is found in *Speier Gebetbuch*, a 1599 publication. Michael Praetorius (1571–1621), one of the most distinguished composers of his time and the greatest master of Protestant church music, harmonized this folk tune and published it in his voluminous *Musae Sioniae* in 1609. Praetorius, who was highly influenced by Italian Baroque music, used the Lutheran chorale texts as the basis for many of his church compositions. "Es ist ein' Ros' entsprungen," a favorite of *a cappella* choirs during the Christmas season, is an example of this Praetorius technique. The inspiration for the carol comes from *Isaiah 11:1* with the words: *"And there shall come forth a rod out of the stem of Jesse, and a Branch shall grow out of his roots."*

GERMAN	ENGLISH
Es ist ein' Ros' entsprungen	Lo, how a rose e'er blooming
Aus einer Wurzel zart,	From tender stem hath sprung,
Wie uns die Alten sungen	Of Jesse's lineage coming,
Aus Jesse kam die Art;	As men of old have sung
Und hat ein Blümlein bracht,	It came a floweret bright
Mitten im kalten Winter,	Amid the cold of winter,
Wohl zu der halben Nacht.	When half spent was the night.
Das Röslein, das ich meine,	Isaiah 'twas foretold it,
Davon Isaias sagt,	The rose I have in mind.
Hat uns gebracht alleine,	With Mary we behold it,
Marie, die reine Magd.	The virgin Mother kind.
Aus Gottes ew'gem Rat	To show God's love aright,
Hat sie ein Kind geboren,	She bore to men a Savior
Wohl su der hablen Nacht.	When half spent was the night.
Das Blümelein, so kleine,	This Flow'r, whose fragrance tender
Das duftet uns so süss;	With sweetness fills the air,
Mit seinem hellen Scheine	Dispels with glorious splendor
Vertreibt's die Finsternis;	The darkness ev'rywhere.
Wahr' Mensch un wahrer Gott,	True man, yet very God;
Hilft uns aus allen Leiden,	From sin and death He saves us,
Rettet von Sünd und Tod.	And lightens ev'ry load.

Facing page:
The Tree of Jesse *(miniature*
from The Salzburg Missal),
Berthold Furtmeyr
(c.1470–1501),
Bayerische Staatsbibliothek,
Munich

7 *The First Nowell*

Other title—
The First Noël

Recording Artists—
Vienna Boys Choir &
The London Symphony
Orchestra

Words & Music—
Anonymous sixteenth-
century English folk

Most often, this beloved carol is spelled "The First Noël," giving rise to the common misconception that the song is of French origin. But "The First Nowell" is the correct spelling. "Nowell" is an English word dating back as far as the fourteenth century, when Geoffrey Chaucer (1340–1400) used the term in his medieval masterpiece *The Canterbury Tales.* Most likely originating from the Cornwall region of southwest England in the sixteenth century, the words for this shepherd song were not published until 1823, and the music until 1833. The origin of the joyous tune remains a mystery; it most likely was the type of Christmas tune that would have been suppressed by the Puritans in the mid-seventeenth century. The refrain of the 1833 melody was revised by the 1870s, with the current smooth notes for the words "Born is the King" replacing an uninspired passage. Over time, "The First Nowell" has become one of the finest of English carols.

For purposes of distinction, the carol "The First Noël" reputedly comes from Cornwall as well, because its lyrics are quite similar to those of "The First Nowell." The word "*noël*" comes from the Latin word *natalis* and is commonly thought of as a French translation for "Christmas carol." Nevertheless, "The First Noel" should not be confused with "The First Nowell." The familiar melody of "The First Noël" was composed by Henry John Gauntlett (1805–1876) in the mid-nineteenth century. Gauntlett, besides being an English composer of some stature, was also an organist and organ designer, music critic, and teacher. Felix Mendelssohn thought very highly of him as a professor of music.

The first Nowell, the angels did say,
Was to certain poor shepherds in fields as they lay;
In fields where they lay a-keeping their sheep,
On a cold winter's night that was so deep.
    REFRAIN:
    Nowell, Nowell, Nowell, Nowell,
    Born is the King of Israel.

They looked up and saw a star,
Shining in the East beyond them far;
And to the earth it gave great light,
And so it continued both day and night.
    REFRAIN:

And by the light of that same star,
Three wise men came from country far;
To seek for a king was their intent,
And to follow the star wheresoever it went.
    REFRAIN:

The Star in the East
*Engraving by R. Brandard
(1805–1862),
Mary Evans Picture Library*

This star drew nigh to the northwest;
O'er Bethlehem it took its rest,
And there it did both stop and stay,
Right o'er the place where Jesus lay.
    REFRAIN:

Then did they know assuredly
Within that house the King did lie:
One entered in then for to see,
And found the babe in poverty.
    REFRAIN:

Then entered in those wise men three,
Fell reverently upon their knee,
And offered there in his presence
Both gold and myrrh and frankincense.
    REFRAIN:

Between an ox-stall and an ass
This child truly there born he was;
For want of clothing they did him lay
All in the manger, among the hay:
    REFRAIN:

Then let us all with one accord
Sing praises to our heavenly Lord,
That hath made heaven and earth of naught,
And with his blood mankind hath bought:
    REFRAIN:

If we in our time shall do well,
We shall be free from death and hell;
For God hath prepared for us all
A resting place in general:
    REFRAIN:

Other Title—
God Rest You Merry

Recording Artists—
RCA Victor Singers; Richard Westenburg, conductor

Words & Music—
Anonymous sixteenth-century English folk

"God Rest Ye Merry, Gentlemen" is one of the best-known carols from England. A cheerful dance tune, it uses a natural minor scale, called a mode in medieval form, that produces a unique and delightful sound effect. The carol probably originates from London and may have first been published by E. F. Rimbault in 1846, although the text was collected by William Sandys in his 1833 volume *Christmas Carols Ancient and Modern*. Since then, other tunes have been found, but this version is believed to be the original. The carol would have been sung by the waits of olden England. Waits were generally municipal employees and watchmen whose specific duties included singing Christmas carols and songs at city or town-sponsored events.

Prior to its publication in 1846, "God Rest Ye Merry, Gentlemen" had gained popularity when it was used in Charles Dickens' famous 1843 story, *A Christmas Carol* (which subsequently became a successful stage play, first in England, and then in the United States).

The year 1843 also marked the beginning of another interesting Christmas custom in England: the creation of the first Christmas greeting card. Soon, Christmas lovers in the United States were emulating yet another English custom. By the 1880s American greeting card companies, such as Louis Prang Co. of Boston, were sponsoring prize-winning contests for illustrators of Christmas cards.

God rest ye merry, Gentlemen,
Let nothing you dismay,
For Jesus Christ our Saviour
Was born on Christmas Day
To save us all from Satan's pow'r,
When we were gone astray.
    REFRAIN:
    O tidings of comfort and joy,
    comfort and joy!
    O tidings of comfort and joy!

In Bethlehem, in Jewry,
This blessed Babe was born,
And laid within a manger
Upon this blessed morn;
To which His mother, Mary,
Did nothing take in scorn.
    REFRAIN:

From God our heav'nly Father
A blessed angel came,
And unto certain shepherds
Brought tidings of the same,
How that in Bethlehem was born
The Son of God by name.
   REFRAIN:

"Fear not," then said the angel,
"Let nothing you affright,
This day is born a Saviour,
Of virtue, power, and might;
So frequently to vanquish all
The friends of Satan quite."
   REFRAIN:

The shepherds at those tidings
Rejoiced much in mind,
And left their flocks afeeding,
In tempest, storm, and wind;
And went to Bethlehem straight away
This blessed Babe to find.
   REFRAIN:

But when to Bethlehem they came,
Whereat this infant lay,
They found Him in a manger,
Where oxen feed on hay;
His mother Mary kneeling,
Unto the Lord did pray.
   REFRAIN:

Now to the Lord sing praises,
All you within this place,
And with true love and brotherhood
Each other now embrace;
This holy tide of Christmas
All others doth efface.
   REFRAIN:

9 ❋ *Good Christian Men, Rejoice*

Recording Artists—
Royal Philharmonic
Orchestra & Chorus;
Peter Knight, conductor

Words—
John Mason Neale
(1818–1866), English
minister, composer, and
translator

Music—
Anonymous fourteenth-
century German hymn

The English version of one of Germany's best-loved carols comes from the 1853 publication, *Carols for Christmastide*. The Rev. John Mason Neale, one of England's great hymn translators, captures the essence of the happy news of the first Christmas by his loose interpretation of "In Dulci Jubilo." The melody of this medieval Latin-German carol may have first appeared in Klug's *Geistliche Lieder* in 1535. Later published in the *Piae Cantiones*, a 1582 book of carols that was one of the finest in Europe, the music may have come from Heinrich Suso (c.1295–1366), a German mystic and Dominican monk.

According to legend, the Blessed Henry Suso was visited by heavenly angels in a dream, danced and sang with them, and then when he awoke immediately wrote down the words and music. However, his own autobiography, *Das Buchlein der ewigen Weisheit* ("The Little Book of Eternal Wisdom"), written in the third person, indicates that some version of the song existed before 1328. Suso supposedly had visionary experiences throughout his life, including a number involving heavenly music. This historical intrigue only adds to the charming nature of the carol.

ENGLISH

Good Christian men, rejoice
With heart and soul and voice!
Give ye heed to what we say;
News! News!
Jesus Christ is born today!
Ox and ass before Him bow,
And He is in the manger now:
Christ is born today!
Christ is born today!

Good Christian men, rejoice
With heart and soul and voice!
Now ye hear of endless bliss
Joy! Joy!
Jesus Christ was born for this!
He hath ope'd the heav'nly door,
And man is blessed evermore:
Christ was born for this!
Christ was born for this!

Used with the tune of these
LATIN-GERMAN lyrics:

In dulci jubilo
Nun singet und seid fro;
Unsers hertzen wonne leit
In praesepio.
Und leuchtet als die sonne
Matris in gremio;
Alpha es et O,
Alpha es et O.

O patris caritas
O nati lenitas,
Wir weren all verloren
Per nostra crimina,
So hat er uns erworken
Coelorum gaudia.
Eya wer wir da,
Eya wer wir da.

Good Christian men, rejoice
With heart and soul and voice.
Now ye need not fear the grave
Peace! Peace!
Jesus Christ was born to save!
Calls you one and calls you all,
To gain His everlasting hall:
Christ was born to save!
Christ was born to save!

Ubi sunt gaudia
Nirgend mehr denn da
Da die engel singen
Nova cantica.
Und die schellen klingen,
In regis curia.
Eya wer wir da,
Eya wer wir da.

Blessed Henry Suso
Francesco de Zurbaran
(1598–1664),
Museo Provincal de Bellas
Artes, Seville

Latin Translations:

In dulci jubilo - in sweet jubilation
In praesepio - in a manger
Matris in gremio - in the mother's lap
Alpha es et O - Thou art the beginning
     and the end
O patris caritas - O love of the Father
O nati lenitas - O gentleness of the Son
Per nostra crimina - by our crimes
Coelorum gaudia - the joys of Heaven
Ubi sunt gaudia - where are the joys?
Nova cantica - new songs
In regis curia - in the court of the King

Recording Artists —
Vienna Boys Choir &
The London Symphony
Orchestra

Words —
John Mason Neale
(1818–1866), English
minister, composer, and
translator

Music —
Anonymous thirteenth-
century northern European

The music for "Good King Wenceslas" comes from a Swedish Spring carol titled "Tempest Adest Floridum," originally found in the 1582 carol book publication *Piae Cantiones*. The English lyrics, some of them quite fanciful and even scorned by critics of John Mason Neale, were based on a story of the nobleman Wenceslas (c.907–929), the Duke of Bohemia, supposedly a kind and good man who was raised by his devoted grandmother. Wenceslas later became king, and during his brief reign he converted his country to Christianity, providing his people with a period of great peace and serenity. He was known to be a just and merciful king, having considerable compassion for the poor and sick, until he was murdered in 929 by an evil younger brother who conspired with other family members and the pagan nobility against him.

The Rev. John Mason Neale, who wrote and published his lyrics in *Carols for Christmas-tide* (1853) for this anonymous thriteenth-century tune, was looking for a good role model for children to emulate. The generous Wenceslas fit the description nicely. "Good King Wenceslas," despite its confounding lyrics, has since become a Christmas favorite for children and adults alike.

ENGLISH

Good King Wenceslas look'd out on
    the feast of Stephen,
When the snow lay round about, deep
    and crisp and even.
Brightly shone the moon that night,
    though the frost was cruel,
When a poor man came in sight,
    gath'ring winter fuel.

"Hither, page, and stand by me,
    if thou know'st it, telling,
Yonder peasant, who is he?
    Where and what his dwelling?
"Sire, he lives a good league hence,
    underneath the mountain;
Right against the forest fence,
    by Saint Agnes' fountain."

"Bring me flesh and bring me wine,
    bring me pine logs hither,
Thou and I will see him dine,
    when we bear him thither."
Page and monarch forth they went,

Used with a tune of LATIN lyrics:

Tempest adest floridum,
furgent manque flores,
Vernales in Omnibus,
imitantur mores,
Hoc quod frigus laeserat,
reparant calores,
Cernimus hoc fieri
per multos labores.

Sunt prata plena floribus,
iucunda aspectu,
Ubi cernere herbae
cum delectu
Gramina et plantae
hyeme quiescunt,
Vernali in tempore virent
et accrescunt.

Haec vobis pulchre
monstrant Deum Creatore,
Quem quoque nos credimus
omnium factorem,
O tempus ergo bilare,

Good King Wenceslas
Engraving from 1871 English carol book

forth they went together,
Through the rude wind's wild lament
    and the bitter weather.

"Sire, the night is darker now,
    and the wind blows stronger.
Fails my heart, I know not how,
    I can go no longer."
"Mark my footsteps, my good page,
    tread thou in them boldly.
Thou shalt find the winter's rage
    freeze thy blood less coldly."

In his master's steps he trod,
    where the snow lay dinted.
Heat was in the very sod
    which the Saint had printed.
Therefore, Christian men, be sure,
    wealth or rank possessing;
Ye who now will bless the poor,
    shall yourselves find blessing.

quo laetari libet,
Renouato nam nundo,
nos nouari decet.

Terra ornatur floribus
et multo decore,
Nos bonestis moribus
et vero amore,
Gaudeamus igitur
tempore iucundo,
Laudemus, Dominum
pectori, ex fundo.

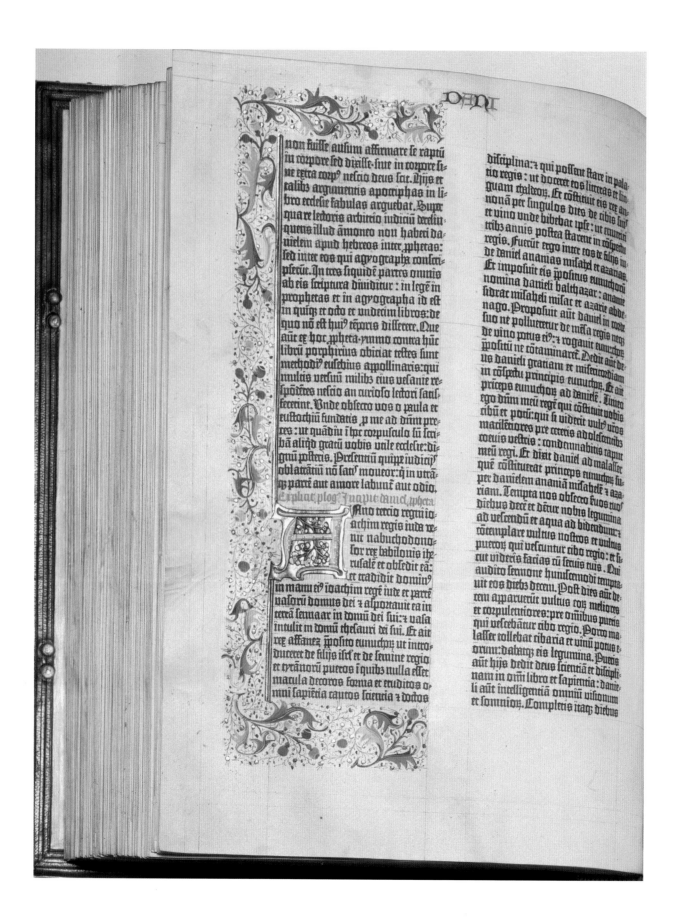

non fuisse ausum affirmare se raptu
in corpore sed dixisse. sive in corpore si
ue extra corp' nescio deus scit. Hijs et
talibz argumentis apocriphas in li
bro ecclesie fabulas arguebat. Supra
qua re lectoris arbitrio iudiciu derelin
quens illud amoneo non haberi da
nielem apud hebreos inter prophetas:
sed inter eos qui agyographa conscri
pserut. In tres siquidem partes omnis
ab eis scriptura diuiditur: in legem in
prophetas et in agyographa id est
in quinq; et octo et undecim libros: de
quo non est hui' temporis disserere. Que
aut ex hoc prophetą. ymmo contra hunc
libru porphirius obiciat testes sunt
methodi' eusebius et appollinaris: qui
multis versuum milibz eius vesanie re
spondetes nescio an curioso lectori satis
fecerint. Vnde obsecro vos o paula et
eustochiu fundatis. p me ad dominu pre
ces: ut quamdiu i hoc corpusculo sum scri
bam aliquid gratu vobis utile ecclesie: di
gnu posteris. Presentiu quippe iudicijs
oblattationu non satis moueor: q in utra
q; parte aut amore labunt aut odio.

Explicit plog'. Incipit daniel prophetą

Anno tercio regni io
achim regis iuda ve
nit nabuchodono
sor rex babilonis ihe
rusalem et obsedit ea:
et tradidit dominus
in manu eius ioachim regem iuda et parte
vasorum domus dei et asportauit ea in
terra sennaar in domum dei sui: et vasa
intulit in domum thesauri dei sui. Et ait
rex asfanez preposito eunuchoru ut intro
duceret de filijs isrł et de semine regio
et tyranorum pueros i quibus nulla esset
macula decoros forma et eruditos om
ni sapientia cautos scientia et doctos

disciplina: et qui possent stare in pala
tio regis: ut doceret eos litteras et lin
guam chaldeor. Et constituit eis rex an
nonam per singulos dies de cibis suis
et vino unde bibebat ipse: ut enutriti
tribz annis postea starent in conspectu
regis. Fuerut ergo inter eos de filijs iu
de daniel ananias misahel et azarias.
Et imposuit eis prepositus eunuchoru
nomina danieli balthazar: ananie
sidrac misaheli misac et azarie abde
nago. Proposuit aut daniel in corde
suo ne polluetur de mesa regis neq;
de vino potus eius: et rogauit eunuchorum
prepositu ne contaminaret. Dedit aut de
us danieli gratiam et misericordiam
in conspectu principis eunuchor. Et ait
princeps eunuchor ad danielem. Timeo
ego dominum meu regem qui constituit vobis
cibu et potu: qui si viderit vultus vestros
macilentiores pre ceteris adolescentibz
coeuis vestris: condennabitis caput
meu regi. Et dixit daniel ad malasar
que constituerat princeps eunuchor. su
per danielem ananiam misahele et aza
riam. Tempta nos obsecro suos tuos
diebus decem et detur nobis legumina
ad vescendum et aqua ad bibendum.
contemplare vultus nostros et vultus
puerorum qui vescuntur cibo regio: et si
cut videris facias cu seruis tuis. Qui
audito sermone huiuscemodi tempta
uit eos diebz decem. Post dies aut de
cem apparuerut vultus eor meliores
et corpulentiores: pre omnibus pueris
qui vescebantur cibo regio. Porro ma
lasar tollebat cibaria et vinu potus e
orum: dabatq; eis legumina. Pueris
aut hijs dedit deus scientia et discipli
nam in omni libro et sapientia: danie
li aut intelligentia omniu visionum
et somnior. Completis itaq; diebus

Recording Artists—
Mormon Tabernacle Choir;
Richard P. Condie,
director/Alexander
Schreiner & Frank Asper,
organ

Words—
Charles Wesley
(1707–1788), English
author and poet

Music—
Felix Mendelssohn
(1809–1847), German com-
poser, conductor, and pianist

"Hark! The Herald Angels Sing" was originally titled "Hymn for Christmas Day" when it was first written as a poem in 1739. The first line, "Hark, how all the welkin rings" ("welkin" in Old English means "heavens"), was changed fourteen years later by George Whitefield (1714–1770), an Anglican clergyman who also co-founded Dartmouth College in Hanover, New Hampshire, for the purpose of educating Indians. More lines of Charles Wesley's poem were revised in later years. Wesley, one of eighteen children born of a modest family, brought his own changes to the original poem by expanding it from four to ten stanzas. Wesley, along with his brother, John Wesley (1703–1791), was an important figure in the founding of Methodism. In addition, he published about 4,430 hymns and wrote thousands more preserved only in manuscript. His most famous collection was *Hymns for the Use of the People Called Methodists.*

William Cummings (1831–1915), an organist at Waltham Abbey, adapted the melody by Felix Mendelssohn to Wesley's hymn and first presented it on Christmas Day in 1855, because he felt the two went nicely together. His arrangement is generally used today. Mendelssohn was commissioned to compose the music for the 1840 Leipzig Gutenberg Festival. Written as a cantata and published as *Festgesang die Kuntstler,* Op. 40, Mendelssohn's music—which eventually became the tune for "Hark! The Herald Angels Sing"—helped to commemorate the 400th anniversary of the invention of the printing press by Johann Gutenberg (c.1400–1468). It accompanied the German lyrics for the second chorus below. Mendelssohn's music was not intended for a carol. The German composer thought the tune had potential as a military or national song, but wrote that "it will never do to sacred words . . . the words must express something gay and popular, as the music tries to do." Fortunately for us, Cummings didn't know about Mendelssohn's doubts and the carol was published in England in 1857, and in the United States a few years later. Against that interesting backdrop, "Hark! The Herald Angels Sing" emerges as one of our more expressively joyful Christmas carols.

ENGLISH

Used with Second Chorus, *"Festgesang: Der Zur Sacularfeier Der Erfindung Buchdruckerkunst"* **of GERMAN lyrics:**

Hark! the herald angels sing,
"Glory to the newborn King!
Peace on earth and mercy mild,
God and sinners reconciled."
Joyful, all ye nations rise,
Join the triumph of the skies;
With the angelic host proclaim,
"Christ is born in Bethlehem!"

Heil ihm! Heil uns!
So schallt zu deinen heil' gen Thronen,
Herr, unser Gott, hinauf der Ruf von
Millionen,
Und brunstig flehen wir:
Lass in des Lichtes Schein der ganzen
Menschheit
Heil, Herr, immermehr gedeih'n.

Facing page:
Page from Gutenberg Bible,
c.1455
The Pierpont Morgan Library

REFRAIN:
    Hark, the herald angels sing,
    "Glory to the newborn King!"

Christ by highest heav'n adored;
Christ the everlasting Lord!
Late in time behold Him come,
Offspring of a Virgin's womb.
Veiled in flesh the Godhead see;
Hail the incarnate Deity.
Pleased as man with man to dwell,
Jesus, our Emmanuel!
    REFRAIN:

Hail the heav'n-born Prince of Peace!
Hail the Son of Righteousness!
Light and life to all He brings,
Ris'n with healing in His wings.
Mild He lays His glory by.
Born that man no more may die.
Born to raise the sons of earth;
Born to give them second birth.
    REFRAIN:

Come Desire of Nations come,
Fix in us Thy Humble home;
Rise the woman's conquering seed,
Bruise in us the serpent's head.
Now display Thy saving power,
Ruin'd nature now restore;
Now in mystic union join
Thine to ours and ours to Thine.
    REFRAIN:

Adam's likeness, Lord, efface;
Stamp Thy image in its place;
Second Adam from above,
Reinstate us in Thy love.
Let us Thee though lost regain,
Then the Life, the Inner Man;
O! to all Thyself impart,
Form'd in each believing heart.
    REFRAIN:

12 ✻ The Holly and the Ivy

Recording Artists—
The Texas Boys Choir; Gregg
Smith Singers; New York
Brass and Percussion
Ensemble; E. Power Biggs,
organ; Gregg Smith,
conductor

Words & Music—
Anonymous late
seventeenth- or early
eighteenth-century
English folk

Although the standard text and tune of this traditional English carol were published in the 1911 volume *English Folk-Carols,* the first strains of "The Holly and the Ivy" may have come from the days of Geoffrey Chaucer (1340–1400), originating from the Somerset and Gloucestershire vicinity.

For centuries, holly and ivy were viewed as important symbols, and they came to be associated particularly with the Christmas season. During the Middle Ages, it was common for homes and churches to be decorated with holly because village folks believed it kept witches and tax-collectors away. Wreaths made from it represented Jesus Christ's crown of thorns and its red berries signified drops of red blood. Ivy was of pagan heritage in keeping with wreaths worn by Bacchus, the Roman wine god. It was common then to dance around evergreen plants that did not die in winter, a practice stemming from the pagan celebration of the Winter Solstice.

Perhaps the genesis of the holly and the ivy goes as far back as St. Augustine (d. 604), when he landed at Kent in 596 A.D. with forty monks to spread Chris-

The Young Bacchus
Caravaggio (1573–1610),
Galleria degli Uffizi, Florence

tianity among the Anglo-Saxons. St. Augustine, who was of noble Roman birth, likely continued the early Roman practice of wreath-giving or decorating hall-ways with garland made from holly for the midwinter feast, Saturnalia. The efforts were so successful that two years later, on Christmas Day, about ten thou-sand men of Kent and their families were baptized into the faith.

In songs of Yuletide, the holly and ivy plants also represented the different genders. The holly was masculine, and the ivy was feminine. Often these sym-bols were used in comical verse. Eventually the holly and the ivy took on much more religious coloration.

Carrying Home the Christmas Holly, *Victorian book illustration, Anonymous, Private Collection*

The holly and the ivy,
When they are both full grown,
Of all the trees that are in the wood,
The holly bears the crown.
>REFRAIN:
>O the rising of the sun
>And the running of the deer,
>The playing of the merry organ,
>Sweet singing in the choir.

The holly bears a blossom
As white as lily flow'r;
And Mary bore sweet Jesus Christ
To be our sweet Savior.
>REFRAIN:

The holly bears a berry
As red as any blood;
And Mary bore sweet Jesus Christ
To do poor sinners good.
>REFRAIN:

The holly bears a prickle
As sharp as any thorn;
And Mary bore sweet Jesus Christ
On Christmas Day in the morn.
>REFRAIN:

The holly bears a bark
As bitter as any gall;
And Mary bore sweet Jesus Christ
For to redeem us all.
>REFRAIN:

13   It Came Upon the Midnight Clear

Other Title—
It Came Upon a Midnight Clear

Recording Artists—
Mormon Tabernacle Choir; Richard P. Condie, director

Words—
Edmund Hamilton Sears (1810–1876), American clergyman

Music—
Richard Storrs Willis (1819–1900), American composer and music critic

Written as a poem by Edmund H. Sears on a cold December day in 1849, "It Came Upon the Midnight Clear" was published that same month in the *Christian Register*, a church magazine. A year later, Richard Storrs Willis wrote a flowing melody under the title "Study No. 23" in his *Church Chorals* and *Choir Studies*, a piece of music that would soon be attached to Sears' lyrics. Willis, an editor and music critic for the *New York Tribune* at the time, had a different hymn in mind when he first composed the music. Later, after he had finished his studies at Yale University, he went on to study music in Europe under the German composer, Felix Mendelssohn.

The Rev. Sears, a farmer's son and direct descendant of one of the original Pilgrim Fathers, was pastor of the Unitarian Church in Wayland, Massachusetts. He loved poems, having begun writing verse at the age of ten and reciting it during his moments of solitude. His poetic carol is particularly noteworthy for its incorporation of the theme of peace among men and nations—a sentiment hardly mentioned in other carols of the day, yet not surprising as the country stood on the brink of civil war. Also, the carol does not make any direct reference to the birth of Christ. Originally five stanzas long, the fourth stanza is generally omitted in most hymnals.

It came upon the midnight clear,
That glorious song of old,
From angels bending near the earth,
To touch their harps of gold:
"Peace on the earth, good will to men,
From heaven's all-gracious King."
The world in solemn stillness lay,
To hear the angels sing.

Still through the cloven skies they come
With peaceful wings unfurled,
And still their heavenly music floats
O'er all the weary world;
Above its sad and lowly plains
They bend on hovering wing,
And ever o'er its Babel sounds
The blessed angels sing.

Yet with the woes of sin and strife
The world hath suffered long;
Beneath the angel-strain have rolled
Two thousand years of wrong;
And man, at war with man, hears not

The love song which they bring;
O hush the noise, ye men of strife,
And hear the angels sing.

O ye, beneath life's crushing load,
Whose forms are bending low,
Who toil along the climbing way
With painful steps and slow,
Look now! for glad and golden hours
Come swiftly on the wing;
O rest beside the weary road
And hear the angels sing!

For lo! the days are hastening on,
By prophet-bards foretold,
When with the ever-circling years
Comes round the age of gold;
When peace shall over all the earth
Its ancient splendors fling,
And the whole world give back the song
Which now the angels sing.

Glad Tidings, c.1880–1885,
American Christmas card,
National Museum of
American History,
Smithsonian Institution

Facing page:
Shout with Joy Ye
Mortals Pray, *Dora Wheeler*
(1858–1940), 1882 American
Christmas card, National
Museum of American History,
Smithsonian Institution

14   *Joy to the World*

Recording Artists—
Royal Philharmonic
Orchestra & Chorus;
Peter Knight, conductor

Words—
Isaac Watts (1674–1748),
English poet and clergyman

Music—
Lowell Mason (1792–1872),
American composer and
music teacher

Another carol written as a poem, "Joy to the World" was the creation of the great hymn composer, Isaac Watts. It was first published in 1719, in *Psalms of David Imitated in the Language of the New Testament.* One of the first tunes that may have been associated with the text was "Antioch" by George Frederic Handel (1685–1759), the famous Baroque composer, as suggested in the 1833 publication *T. Hawkes Collection of Tunes.* However, a number of other composers have also been connected with this tune, thus bringing some measure of doubt that Handel arranged it.

Lowell Mason, the leading Presbyterian hymn-composer in the United States, first united his magnificent tune with Watts' text in 1836. The two have since been inseparable. Watts may have found inspiration for his poem from *Psalm 98:4-9* of the Old Testament, particularly the verse lines, *"Make a joyful noise unto the Lord, all the earth."* A popular carol that has become a staple among Christmas offerings, "Joy to the World" bursts forth in exuberant, hopeful, and triumphant notes about the good news of Christ's birth.

Joy to the world! the Lord has come;
Let earth receive her King.
Let ev'ry heart prepare His room,
And heav'n and nature sing,
And heav'n and nature sing,
And heav'n, and heav'n and nature sing.

Joy to the world! the Savior reigns:
Let men their songs employ,
While fields and floods, rocks, hills and plains
Repeat the sounding joy,
Repeat the sounding joy,
Repeat, repeat the sounding joy.

He rules the world with truth and grace,
And makes the nations prove
The glories of His righteousness
And wonders of His love,
And wonders of His love,
And wonders, wonders of His love.

Les Anges dans nos campagnes

English Title—
Angels We Have Heard
on High

Recording Artists—
Vienna Boys Choir &
The London Symphony
Orchestra

Words & Music —
Anonymous eighteenth-
century French folk

The text and fine melody of "Les Anges dans nos campagnes," possibly based on a traditional French *noël*, come from either Lorraine or Provence. However, the melody of the refrain could be considerably older, perhaps dating back to the fourteenth or fifteenth century, when a number of macaronic carols were composed. Macaronic carols consisted of both vernacular and Latin lyrics, a combination required to please musically sensitive Church officials who were still committed to the monopoly of Latin.

"Les Anges dans nos campagnes" may have been first published in *Choix de cantiques sur des airs nouveaux*, a 1842 publication. The French text originally had eight stanzas, although in subsequent publications it might number five or fewer. The English text, "Angels We Have Heard on High," a loose translation by James Chadwick (1813–1882), numbered only four stanzas, one of which appeared in the 1864 London publication *Crown of Jesus Music.* The first printing of the English text, however, appeared in Chadwick's own *Holy Family Hymns* four years earlier. The version with which we are now familiar was printed in a 1916 volume, *Carols Old and Carols New.* The tune for "Les Anges dans nos campagnes" was also used by James Montgomery (1771–1854), a Scottish newspaper editor, for his carol composition "Angels from the Realms of Glory."

The refrain "Gloria in excelsis Deo" is also the title of the Latin song, known as "The Angels Hymn," that was sung as part of a 129 A.D. religious observance of the Nativity at the behest of Telephorus, a Greek and the seventh pope of the early Christian Church.

The literal translation of this *noël* means "angels in our mountains." Tradition has it that on Christmas Eve the shepherds in southern France would sing the angel's song, "Gloria in excelsis Deo," to each other from their respective hilltops. This charming practice probably began during the Middle Ages in commemoration of the coming of the Christ Child.

FRENCH	ENGLISH
Les anges dans nos campagnes	Angels we have heard on high,
Ont entonné l'hymne des cieux,	Sweetly singing o'er the plains,
Et l'écho de nos montagnes	And the mountains in reply
Redit ce chant mélodieux:	Echo back their joyous strains.
REFRAIN:	REFRAIN:
Gloria in excelsis Deo.	*Gloria in excelsis Deo.*
Gloria in excelsis Deo!	*Gloria in excelsis Deo!*
Bergers, pur qui cette fête?	Shepherds, why this jubilee?
Quel est l'objet de tous ces chants?	Why your joyous strains prolong?
'Quel valinqueur, quelle conquète	Say what may the tidings be,
Mérite ces cris triomphants?	Which inspire your heav'nly song.
REFRAIN:	REFRAIN:

Annunciation to the
Shepherds, c.1510–1515
(*from* Les Belles Heures de
Jean Duc de Berry),
Metropolitan Museum of Art

Ils annoncent la naissance
Du libérateur d'Israël,
Et, pleins de reconnaissance,
Chantent en ce jour solennel:
    REFRAIN:
Bergers, loin de vos retraites
Unissez-vous à leurs concerts
Et que vos tendres musettes
Fassent retentir dans les airs:
    REFRAIN:
Cherons tous l'heureux village
Qui l'a vu naître sous ses toits,
Offrons-lui le tendre hommage
Et de nos coeurs et nos voix!
    REFRAIN:

Come to Bethlehem and see Him
Whose birth the angels sing;
Come, adore on bended knee
Christ the Lord, the newborn King.
    REFRAIN:
See Him in a manger laid
Whom the angels praise above;
Mary, Joseph, lend your aid,
While we raise our hearts in love.
    REFRAIN:

Latin Translation:

Gloria in excelsis Deo -
Glory to God in the highest

16   O Little Town of Bethlehem

Recording Artists—
RCA Victor Singers; Richard
Westenburg, conductor

Words—
Phillips Brooks
(1835–1893),
American minister

Music—
Lewis Henry Redner
(1831–1908), American
church organist and
real-estate executive

One of America's most beloved carols, "O Little Town of Bethlehem," was written as a poem by Phillips Brooks in 1868, when he was a young rector in Philadelphia, just three years after he had traveled to the Holy Land. There he was impressed by Christmas Eve services at the Church of the Nativity in Bethlehem. That night, as he sat on a hill looking back at the village, while shepherds watched their flocks, he felt at peace with himself. He later told friends, "That experience was so overpowering that forever there will be a singing in my soul." Reverend Brooks persuaded Lewis Redner, the church organist, to set his poem to music.

Redner put off composing the music until the very last moment; then during the night, he had a dream that inspired him to begin work on his composition. Immediately upon arising, he wrote down the melody and offered it to the children the following morning. "O Little Town of Bethlehem" has since attained a lofty status in the international repertoire of traditional Christmas carols, and the tolling of its lyrics brings enchantment to the sacred story about a glorious starry night of long ago.

O little town of Bethlehem,
How still we see Thee lie!
Above the deep and dreamless sleep,
The silent stars go by;
Yet in thy dark streets shineth
The everlasting Light;
The hopes and fears of all the years
Are met in Thee tonight.

For Christ is born of Mary,
And gathered all above,
While mortals sleep, the angels keep,
Their watch of wondering love.
O morning stars, together
Proclaim the holy birth!
And praises sing to God the King,
And peace to men on earth.

How silently, how silently,
The wondrous gift is giv'n!
So God imparts to human hearts
The blessings of His heav'n.
No ear may hear His coming,
But in this world of sin,
Where meek souls will receive Him, still
The dear Christ enters in.

Church of the Nativity, *1840*
David Roberts (1796–1864)
Paisley Museum & Art Galleries

Where children pure and happy
Pray to the blessed Child,
Where misery cries out to Thee,
Son of the mother mild;
Where charity stands watching
And faith holds wide the door,
The dark night wakes, the glory breaks,
And Christmas comes once more.

O holy Child of Bethlehem!
Descend to us, we pray;
Cast out our sin and enter in,
Be born in us today.
We hear the Christmas angels
The great glad tidings tell;
O come to us, abide with us,
Our Lord Immanuel.

17 ✳ *O Tannenbaum*

English Titles—
O Christmas Tree;
Oh Christmas Tree

Recording Artists—
Marilyn Horne, mezzo-soprano; Mormon Tabernacle Choir; Columbia Symphony Orchestra; Jerold Ottley, conductor

Words—
Anonymous sixteenth-or seventeenth-century German folk for first verse; Ernest Gebhard Anschutz (1800–1861), German schoolmaster and lyricist for other verses

Music—
Anonymous sixteenth-or seventeenth-century German folk

"O Tannenbaum," perhaps the best-known carol from Germany, specifically refers to the Christmas tree, a much-celebrated symbol in tradition and song in Germany since the fifteenth and sixteenth centuries. Representing loyalty and fresh life, which was especially appreciated during winter's darkest days, the tradition of a Christmas tree dates back to the days of the Roman Empire when the evergreen was used in a decorative fashion during the period of the Winter Solstice in late December and early January.

The evergreen was also used by Germans for pagan rituals celebrated at other times of the year, such as for St. Urban's Ritt on May 25th in the city of Nuremberg, once a pagan stronghold. This is understandable because the symbol of the evergreen was well rooted in the old religions of central Europe before they were totally eradicated by the early Christian Church.

St. Boniface (c.680–755), English apostle to the Germans, supposedly brought the custom of decorating evergreen trees with him. Martin Luther has also been credited with beginning the custom in the sixteenth century, and because of his association with it, parts of Protestant Europe adopted the practice. During his lifetime, in 1539, a Christmas tree was used for the first time in the Strasbourg Cathedral.

The earliest printed reference to decorating Christmas trees was a 1561 Alsatian ordinance that dictated how large an evergreen bush must be before it could be cut down. Over the years the custom spread to the United States and Canada and became a firmly established tradition. Several legends have sprung from the tree trimming practice, including one that relates how all the trees of the world bore their best fruit on the night the Christ Child was born.

The original "O Tannenbaum" is believed to have had only one verse, the text of which appeared in the 1820 publication *Weisenbuch zu den Volksliedern fur Volksschulen.* Two additional verses were added by Ernest Gebhard Anschutz in 1824 for his school children to sing, as Christmas trees had become more common in his town of Leipzig. The melody belonged to an old Latin song that had been sung by German students for many generations prior to Anschutz's creation, having been published in 1799 in *Melodien zum Mildheimischen Liederbuch.* The music has also been adopted for a number of different texts, including the song "Maryland, My Maryland." George K. Evans (b.1917), coauthor of the well-researched 1963 text, *The International Book of Christmas Carols,* provides the English translation.

GERMAN	ENGLISH
O Tannenbaum, O Tannenbaum,	O Christmas tree, O Christmas tree,
Wie treu sind deine Blätter!	With faithful leaves unchanging.
O Tannenbaum, O Tannenbaum,	O Christmas tree, O Christmas tree,
Wie treu sind deine Blätter!	With faithful leaves unchanging.
Du grünst nicht nur zur Sommerzeit,	Not only green in summer's heat,

Nein, auch im Winter, wenn es schneit,
O Tannenbaum, O Tannenbaum,
Wie treu sind deine Blätter!

O Tannenbaum, O Tannenbaum,
Du kannst mir sehr gefallen!
O Tannenbaum, O Tannenbaum,
Du kannst mir sehr gefallen!
Wie oft hat mich zur Weihnachtszeit
Ein Baum von dir mich hoch erfreut!
O Tannenbaum, O Tannenbaum,
Du kannst mir sehr gefallen!

O Tannenbaum, O Tannenbaum,
Dein Kleid will mich was lehren!
O Tannenbaum, O Tannenbaum,
Dein Kleid will mich was lehren!
Die Hoffnung und Beständigkeit
Gibt Trost und Kraft zu aller Zeit.
O Tannenbaum, O Tannenbaum,
Dein Kleid will mich was lehren!

But also winter's snow and sleet,
O Christmas tree, O Christmas tree,
With faithful leaves unchanging.

O Christmas tree, O Christmas tree,
Of all the trees most lovely;
O Christmas tree, O Christmas tree,
Of all the trees most lovely.
Each year, you bring me to delight
Gleaming in the Christmas night.
O Christmas tree, O Christmas tree,
Of all the trees most lovely.

O Christmas tree, O Christmas tree,
Your leaves will teach me, also,
O Christmas tree, O Christmas tree,
Your leaves will teach me, also.
That hope and love and faithfulness
Are precious things I can possess.
O Christmas tree, O Christmas tree,
Your leaves will teach me, also.

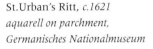

St.Urban's Ritt, *c.1621*
aquarell on parchment,
Germanisches Nationalmuseum

18 *Stille Nacht, heilige Nacht*

English Titles—
Silent Night, Holy Night;
Silent Night;
Holy Night

Recording Artists—
Mormon Tabernacle Choir;
Alexander Schreiner &
Frank Asper, organ

Words—
Joseph Mohr (1792–1848),
Austrian Catholic priest

Music—
Franz Gruber (1787–1863),
Austrian church organist
and composer

Perhaps the best-known Christmas carol of all time, having been translated in forty-four different languages, "Stille Nacht, heilige Nacht" ("Silent Night") has an interesting story about its creation. On Christmas Eve in 1818, Franz Gruber, the church organist, had to quickly rearrange the planned music after the organ of his small village church, St. Nicholas in Obendorf, Austria, had broken down. Needing music to go along with the poetic lyrics of Rev. Joseph Mohr, a Catholic priest, the organist composed a melody for two solo voices, a chorus, and guitar. As a result of the creative labors of both pastor and organist, the Christmas music repertoire was rewarded with what would become one of our most devotional carols.

The source of inspiration for Rev. Mohr's poem—probably written two years earlier when the priest was in the service of another parish church in Austria—is open to some speculation. But one account with a plausible ring to it suggests a humble scenario.

Accordingly, the Rev. Mohr was visited by a villager who came to announce the birth of a child in the house of a young woodsman. At the behest of the anxious father, the priest quickly plodded through the snow to bring words of good cheer and blessings for the young mother and the house. The Rev. Mohr, though weary from the trek through the heavy snow, was quite impressed by the pervasive and comforting silence, the snow, and the starry night. Upon his arrival at the woodsman's humble abode he was further moved when he gazed upon the small, rough-hewn cradle where the baby lay and the woodchopper tending to his wife at a nearby bed of pine logs.

The priest was transfixed by the scene and overcome by a feeling of radiance and holiness about the place. It struck him that the surroundings bore a strong resemblance to how the birth of another child, the Infant Jesus, had been described eighteen hundred years earlier. After blessing the woodsman's home, the Rev. Mohr returned to his study and began reflecting on the scene he had just witnessed. While looking out across the snowy mountains and stars, he murmured to himself, "Silent Night, Holy Night." In this holy mood, he may have written the simple words of six stanzas that softly proclaimed the joy and peace of the first Christmas.

Six or seven years after its initial church performance, an organ repairman, hired to reconstruct the organ at St. Nicholas Church, found a copy of the carol at the church and received permission to take it home with him. Soon after, traveling singing groups began to sing "Stille Nacht, heilige Nacht" in different parts of Austria and ultimately in other regions of the world, further spreading the carol's popularity. The song would become exceptionally popular in the United States after World War I, when returning war veterans remembered hearing it sung by German soldiers during Christmas truces.

*Holy Night (from a triptych),
Fritz von Uhde (1848–1911),
Sachsische Landesbibliothek-
Staats-und
Universitatsbibliothek, Dresden*

For a time, the carol was thought to be either of anonymous origin or from the hand of Johann Michael Haydn (1737–1806), who was noted for his compositions of sacred music (as well as for being the brother of the more famous Joseph Haydn). The carol was probably first published in the 1838–1840 period, in a collection of "four genuine Tyrolean songs." One English translation reduced it to three stanzas, and a widely accepted version was completed in 1863 by the Rev. John Freeman Young (1820–1885), who later served as the Episcopal bishop of Florida in 1867.

The wonderful result of these developments was a simple, loving, tender song, resonating even today with the true meaning of Christmas. Is it any surprise, then, that "Silent Night" now ranks as the most-recorded song in history?

GERMAN	ENGLISH

GERMAN

Stille Nacht, heilige Nacht!
Alles schläft, einsam wacht
Nur das traute, hochheilige Paar.
Holder Knab im lockigen Haar:
 Schlaf in himmlischer Ruh!
 Schlaf in himmlischer Ruh!

Stille Nacht, heilige Nacht!
Gottes Sohn, o wie lacht
Lieb' aus deinem göttlichen Mund
Da uns schlägt die rettende Stund:
 Jesus in Deiner Geburt!
 Jesus in Deiner Geburt!

Stille Nacht, heilige Nacht!
Die der Welt Heil gebracht;
Aus des Himmels goldenen Höh'n
Uns der Gnaden Fulle lässt seh'n:
 Jesum in Menschengestalt!
 Jesum in Menschengestalt!

Stille Nacht, heilige Nacht!
Wo sich heut' alle Macht
Väterlicher Liebe ergoss
Und als Bruder huldvoll umschloss
 Jesus die Volker der Welt!
 Jesus die Volker der Welt!

Stille Nacht, heilige Nacht!
Lange schön uns bedacht,
Als der Herr vom Grimme befreit
In der Väter urgrauen Zeit
 Aller Welt Schonung verhiess!
 Aller Welt Schonung verhiess!

Stille Nacht, heilige Nacht!
Hirten erst kund gemacht,
Durch der Engel "Hallelujah!"
Tönt es laut von fern und nah:
 "Jesus der Retter ist da!"
 "Jesus der Retter ist da!"

ENGLISH

Silent night, holy night,
All is calm, all is bright;
Round yon virgin mother and Child,
Holy Infant so tender and mild,
Sleep in heavenly peace,
Sleep in heavenly peace.

Silent night, holy night,
Shepherds quake at the sight;
Glories stream from heaven afar,
Heavenly hosts sing *Alleluia*:
Christ, the Saviour, is born!
Christ, the Saviour, is born!

Silent night, holy night,
Son of God, Love's pure light;
Radiance beams from Thy holy face,
With the dawn of redeeming grace,
Jesus, Lord, at Thy birth.
Jesus, Lord, at Thy birth.

Facing page:
A Twelfth Night Feast
Jan Steen (1626–1679),
Museum of Fine Arts, Boston

74 ∾

The Twelve Days of Christmas

Other Titles—
*The First Day of Christmas;
On the First Day of
Christmas*

Recording Artists—
*Mormon Tabernacle Choir;
Richard P. Condie, director;
New York Philharmonic
Orchestra; Leonard
Bernstein, conductor*

Words & Music—
*Anonymous seventeenth-
or eighteenth-century
English folk*

The traditional twelve days of Christmas extend from Christmas Day to the Epiphany, or from December 25 to January 6 (the Twelfth Night) of the new year. "The Twelve Days of Christmas" was meant to be sung during this period, but in the United States it generally is not sung at all after Christmas Day. In fact, hardly any Christmas music, religious or secular, is heard in the United States after December 25. Since a number of carols were intended to celebrate post-Christmas feast days, including the Epiphany—January 6, the date for honoring the visitation of the Magi (Wise Men)—it would be a nice practice to revive singing carols during this period.

Possibly written around 1700 and quite likely based on a similar French song, "The Twelve Days of Christmas" first appeared in the 1780 publication *Mirth without Mischief* in England. The song was intended as a children's memory game. The first child recited the first verse, the second child recited the next, and so on until one player missed the verse for which a penalty had to be paid.

Recreating the festive air of secular carols from the early Renaissance era, it has been adapted to a number of lyrical settings. A recent account, perhaps more myth than fact, relates that because there was persecution of Catholics in England around the time, "The Twelve Days of Christmas" was created as a catechism song for young Catholics to help them remember the lessons of their faith. Thus, "true love" referred to God. The "partridge in a pear tree" was Jesus Christ, symbolized as a mother partridge feigning injury to protect her helpless young from predators. The "me" who receives the presents signifies every baptized person. The symbols of "The Twelve Days of Christmas" were thus represented as follows:

1 partridge in a pear tree: Jesus Christ
2 turtle doves: the Old and New Testaments
3 French hens: faith, hope & charity
4 colly birds: the four Gospels
5 gold rings: the first five books of the Old Testament
6 geese a-laying: the six days of creation
7 swans a-swimming: the seven gifts of the Holy Spirit
8 maids a-milking: the eight Beatitudes
9 ladies dancing: nine fruits of the Holy Spirit
10 lords a-leaping: the Ten Commandments
11 pipers piping: the eleven faithful disciples
12 drummers drumming: the twelve beliefs in the Apostles' Creed.

Today the song retains its good nature and popularity in many parts of the English-speaking world.

On the first day of Christmas my true love gave to me,
    A partridge in a pear tree.

On the second day of Christmas my true love gave to me,
    Two turtle doves and a partridge in a pear tree.

On the third day of Christmas my true love gave to me,
    Three French hens, two turtle doves, and a
    partridge in a pear tree.

On the fourth day of Christmas my true love gave to me,
    Four colly birds, three French hens, two turtle
    doves, and a partridge in a pear tree.

On the fifth day of Christmas my true love gave to me,
    Five gold rings, four colly birds, three French
    hens, two turtle doves, and a partridge in a
    pear tree.

On the sixth day of Christmas my true love gave to me,
Six geese a-laying, five gold rings, four colly
birds, three French hens, two turtle doves, and
a partridge in a pear tree.

On the seventh day of Christmas my true love gave to me,
Seven swans a-swimming, six geese a-laying, five
gold rings, four colly birds, three French hens,
two turtle doves, and a partridge in a pear tree.

On the eighth day of Christmas my true love gave to me,
Eight maids a-milking, seven swans a-swimming,
six geese a-laying, five gold rings, four colly
birds, three French hens, two turtle doves, and
a partridge in a pear tree.

On the ninth day of Christmas my true love gave to me,
Nine ladies dancing, eight maids a-milking, seven
swans a-swimming, six geese a-laying, five gold
rings, four colly birds, three French hens, two
turtle doves, and a partridge in a pear tree.

On the tenth day of Christmas my true love gave to me,
Ten lords a-leaping, nine ladies dancing, eight
maids a-milking, seven swans a-swimming, six geese
a-laying, five gold rings, four colly birds, three
French hens, two turtle doves, and a partridge in
a pear tree.

On the eleventh day of Christmas my true love gave to me,
Eleven drummers drumming, ten lords a-leaping, nine
ladies dancing, eight maids a-milking, seven swans
a-swimming, six geese a-laying, five gold rings,
four colly birds, three French hens, two turtle
doves, and a partridge in a pear tree.

On the twelfth day of Christmas my true love gave to me,
Twelve pipers piping, eleven drummers drumming, ten
lords a-leaping, nine ladies dancing, eight maids
a-milking, seven swans a-swimming, six geese
a-laying, five gold rings, four colly birds, three
French hens, two turtle doves, and a partridge
in a pear tree.

Other Titles—
Veni, Immanuel;
Veni, Veni, Emmanuel

English Title—
O Come, O Come,
Emmanuel

Recording Artists—
RCA Victor Singers;
Richard Westenburg,
conductor

Words & Music—
Anonymous twelfth-
or thirteenth-century
European hymn,
possibly French

"Veni, Emmanuel" is possibly the oldest of our more notable carol hymns. In some quarters, it is believed that monastery monks composed the original hymn of seven verses. They would sing one verse per day at *Vespers*, the late afternoon or early evening canonical hour of prayer, for seven straight days prior to Christmas Eve.

The music may have evolved over the years from Gregorian plainsongs (chant), based on several plainsong phrases of the *Kyrie* that were supposedly found in ancient French missals. The original words—possibly Latin antiphons known as the *Seven Greater Antiphons*, or *Great "O" Antiphons of Advent*, because each of them began with the interjection *"O"* for the Messiah as he was addressed in various *Old Testament* texts—may date from the ninth century, or earlier. However, the Latin lyrics of this carol can only be definitely traced back to 1710.

The English conversion, "O Come, O Come, Emmanuel," was the creation of Rev. John Mason Neale (1818–1866), an eccentric Anglican priest with Catholic proclivities, who was also a composer and translator. Neale's first translation was produced in 1851. Two years later, he wrote another one with altered text.

Another Anglican, Thomas Helmore (1811–1890), produced a haunting melody three years later in *Hymnal Noted* to go with Neale's 1851 translation, and for the next twenty-two years a number of other settings were composed. Supposedly, Helmore changed some plainsongs from the twelfth or thirteenth century, but the oldest known predecessor is a fifteenth-century processional used by Franciscan nuns. Because of his expertise in plainsong and Gregorian chant, Helmore was closely associated with the Rev. Neale and complemented Neale's scholarly work with ancient Greek and Latin texts.

In 1906, Thomas Alexander Lacey (1853–1931) produced another English version. Today, "Veni, Emmanuel" is generally sung in four or fewer stanzas, and it is rare to find a hymnal carrying all seven stanzas. But there is no doubt that the possibly long and storied evolution of this beloved carol hymn has provided us with a sacred and exceptional Christmas gift.

LATIN	ENGLISH
Veni, veni Emmanuel	O come, O come, Emmanuel,
Captivum solve Israel,	And ransom captive Israel
Qui gemit in exilio	That mourns in lonely exile here
Privatus Dei Filio.	Until the Son of God appear.
REFRAIN:	REFRAIN:
Gaude, gaude, Emmanuel,	Rejoice, rejoice! Emmanuel
Nascetur pro te Israel.	Shall come to thee O Israel.
Veni, O jesse virgula	O come, thou Rod of Jesse, free
Ex hostis tuos ungula,	Thine own from Satan's tyranny.
De specu tuos tartari	From depths of hell thy people save
Educ, et antro barathri.	And give them victory o'er the grave.
REFRAIN:	REFRAIN:

The Angels Serve Food
to the Monks,
Fra Angelico (1387–1455),
The Louvre

Veni, veni O Oriens	O come, thou dayspring, come and cheer
Solare nos adveniens,	Our spirits by thine advent here;
Noctis depelle nebulas	Disperse the gloomy shades of night
Dirasque noctis tenebras.	And death's dark shadows put to flight.
REFRAIN:	REFRAIN:
Veni Clavis davidica	O come, thou Key of David, come
Fegna reclude caelica	And open wide our heavenly home;
Fac iter tutum superum	Make safe the way that leads on high,
Et claude vias inferum.	And close the path to misery.
REFRAIN:	REFRAIN:
Veni, O Sapientia,	O come, thou Wisdom from on high,
Quae hic disponis omnia;	Who orderest all things mightily;
Veni, viam prudentiae	To us the path of knowledge show,
Ut doceas et gloriae.	And teach us in her ways to go.
REFRAIN:	REFRAIN:
Veni, veni, Adonai,	O come, O come, thou Lord of might,
Qui populo in Sinai	Who to thy tribes on Sinai's height
Legem dedisti vertice	In ancient times didst give the law,
In majestate gloriae.	In cloud, and majesty, and awe.
REFRAIN:	REFRAIN:
Veni, veni, Rex gentium	O come, Desire of nations, bind
Veni, Redemptor omnium,	In one the hearts of all mankind;
Ut salvas tuos famulos	Bid thou our sad divisions cease,
Peccati sibi conscios.	And be thyself our King of Peace.
REFRAIN:	REFRAIN:

—Carol based on the *Great "O" Antiphons of Advent:*

December 17: (from *Ecclesiastes 24:5*)

O Sapientia quae ex ore Altissimi prodiisti, attingens a fine usque ad finem, fortiter suaviterque disponens omnia: veni ad docendum nos viam prudentiae.

O Wisdom, You came forth from the mouth of the Most High, and reaching from beginning to end, You ordered all things mightily and sweetly. Come, and teach us the way of prudence!

December 18: (from *Exodus 6:13*)

O Adonai, et Dux domus Israel, qui Moysi in igne flammae rubi apparuisti, et ei in Sina legem dedisti: veni ad tedimendum nos in bracchio extento.

O Adonai and Ruler of the house of Israel, You appeared to Moses in the fire of the burning bush, and on Mount Sinai gave him Your Law. Come, with an outstretched arm redeem us!

December 19: (from *Isaiah 11:10*)

O radix Jesse, qui stas in signum populorum, super quem continebunt reges os suum, quem gentes deprecabuntur: veni ad liberandum nos, iam noli tardare.

O Root of Jesse, You stand for an ensign of mankind; before You kings shall keep silence, and to You all nations shall have recourse. Come, save us, and do not delay.

December 20: (from *Isaiah 22:22* and *Apocalypse 3:7*)

O clavis David, et sceptrum domus Israel; qui aperis, et nemo claudit; claudis, et nemo aperit: veni, et educ vinctum de domo carceris, sedentem in tenebris, et umbra mortis.

O Key of David and Scepter of the house of Israel: You open and no man closes; You close and no man opens. Come, and deliver him from the chains of prison who sits in darkness and in the shadows of death.

December 21: (from *Zacharias 6:12*)

O Oriens, splendor lucis aeternae, et sol iustitiae: veni, et illumina cedentes in tenebris, et umbra mortis.

O Rising Dawn, Radiance of the Light eternal and Sun of Justice; come, and enlighten those who sit in darkness and in the shadow of death.

December 22: (from *Aggeus 2:8*)

O Rex gentium, et desideratus earum, lapisque angularis, qui facis utraque unum: veni, et salva hominem, quem de limo formasti.

O King of the Gentiles, and the Desired of all, You are the cornerstone that binds two into one. Come, and save poor man whom You fashioned out of clay.

December 23: (from *Isaiah 7:14* and *8:8*)

O Emmanuel, Rex et legifer noster, exspectatio gentium, et Salvator earum: veni ad salvandum nos, Domine Deus noster.

O Emmanuel, our King and Lawgiver, the Expected of nations and their Savior: Come, and save us, O Lord our God!

Other Titles—
Here We Come A-Caroling;
Here We Come
A-Wassailing

Recording Artists—
Mormon Tabernacle Choir;
Richard P. Condie, director

Words & Music—
Anonymous seventeenth-
century English folk

A traditional English tune, probably originating from Yorkshire, the "Wassail Song" is one of very good cheer. The full, eight-stanza text comes from W. H. Husk's 1864 carol collection, *Songs of the Nativity.*

The word "wassail" is a salutation meaning "to drink to one's health," and the reply to this salutation would be "drink hail!" The practice may go back to the fifth century, although the first mention of it appeared much later, in 1140. Its roots most likely come from an early dance form in northern England. During the Christmas season, carolers traveled from house to house, bringing good wishes and carrying an empty bowl. The master of the house being wassailed was expected to fill the bowl with hot, spicy ale. Children were treated especially well as they went door to door, similar to American children at Halloween, seeking holiday goodies in return for their caroling and dancing.

Here we come a-caroling
Among the leaves so green;
Here we come a-wand'ring
So fair to be seen.
    REFRAIN:
    Love and joy come to you,
    And to you glad Christmas too,
    And God bless you and send you a Happy New Year,
    And God send you a Happy New Year.

Our wassail cup is made
Of the rosemary tree,
And so is your beer
Of the best barley.
    REFRAIN:

We are not daily beggars
That beg from door to door,
But we are neighbors' children
Whom you have seen before.
    REFRAIN:

Call up the butler of this house,
Put on his golden ring;
Let him bring us a glass of beer,
And better we shall sing.
    REFRAIN:

We have got a little purse
Of stretching leather skin;
We want a little of your money

Lady of the Manor Offers
Wassail Bowl to Carol
Singers, *Engraving by*
R. W. Buss (1804–1875),
Mary Evans Picture Library

Facing page:
The Three Wise Men, *c.1878*
John La Farge (1835–1910),
Museum of Fine Arts, Boston

To line it well within.
 REFRAIN:

Bring us out a table,
And spread it with a cloth;
Bring us out a moldy cheese,
And some of your Christmas loaf.
 REFRAIN:

God bless the master of this house,
Likewise the mistress too;
And all the little children
That round the table go.
 REFRAIN:

Good Master and good Mistress
While you sit by the fire,
Pray think of us poor children
Who are wandering in the mire.
 REFRAIN:

22 ✳ *We Three Kings of Orient Are*

Recording Artists—
RCA Victor Singers; Richard
Westenburg, conductor

Words & Music—
John Henry Hopkins
(1820–1891), American
minister, composer, music
teacher, and designer of
stained glass windows

"We Three Kings of Orient Are" is one of the few carols whose theme is primarily about the visit of the Kings, or Wise Men, to the Christ Child in Bethlehem. Written in 1857 by the Reverend John Henry Hopkins, "Kings of Orient," its original title, was later published in 1863 in his popular work *Carols, Hymns, and Songs*. It quickly gained recognition outside the United States, especially in England, where it was the only American carol published in *Christmas Carols, New and Old*, a landmark 1871 collection that played a major role in reviving carol collecting and singing in England.

Hopkins wrote the carol as a Christmas gift for his nieces and nephews while he was in New York serving, among other things, as an instructor of church music for the General Theological Seminary there. Because the music has an ar-

chaic flavor, the carol is often thought to be older than it actually is. Plus, the unique structure of Hopkins' carol allowed the kings to have direct speech and an opportunity for drama.

The journey of the Three Kings as Wise Men, or Magi from the word *"magoi,"* appears in the *New Testament* in *St. Matthew 2:1–11.* The Magi was a class of priestly astrologers and magicians of Persia. Some suggestions about the Magi and the Star of Bethlehem came from the *Old Testament,* namely passages from *Psalms 68:29-31, Isaiah 49:7, 60:3,6,10,* and *Numbers 24:17.*

During the early days of the Christian Church, the exotic story of the Three Kings caught popular imagination, and the three acquired names: 1) Caspar (or Gaspar), the King of Tarsus; 2) Melchior, the King of Arabia and Nubia; and 3) Balthazar, the King of Saba (or Sheba). One of the first images of them, depicting them as part of a crèche scene worshipping the Christ Child, appeared in the 4th century as a painting on a sarcophagus, now located in the Basilica of Saint Maximim, France. Since then they have continued to be so honored and have become a permanent part of Christmas lore.

An interesting custom has developed over the years regarding the Three Kings. Each year, after the heads of households have received their first Christmas card with a picture of the Three Kings on it, it is tacked over the front entrance of the house. This custom had its origins in Europe, where for centuries, on the day of the Epiphany, or January 6th, parish churches blessed and distributed water and chalk for the blessing of homes.

The water was used in remembrance of Baptism. The chalk was used to mark over the front door the initials of the Three Kings and the numerals of the new year, e.g., 19+C+M+B+99 (for the year 1999), or 20+C+M+B+00 (for the year 2000). From the greatest palaces to the humblest hovels, the chalk marks would be the same for all households. These markings were intended to lead the Three Kings, should they return, to easily find where Christ would be—in the hearts and minds of everyone.

From the wealth of Christmas stories surrounding the Three Kings, it is understandable where Hopkins would have looked for his inspiration.

We three kings of Orient are,   **(sung by The Three Kings)**
Bearing gifts we traverse afar
Field and fountain, moor and mountain,
Following yonder star.
    REFRAIN:
    O Star of wonder, Star of might,
    Star with royal beauty bright,
    Westward leading, still proceeding,
    Guide us to Thy perfect light.

Born a King on Bethlehem's plain,   (sung by *Melchior*)
Gold I bring to crown Him again;
King forever, ceasing never
Over us all to reign.
     REFRAIN:

Frankincense to offer have I,   (sung by *Gaspar*)
Incense owns a Deity nigh;
Prayer and praising, all men raising,
Worship Him, God on high.
     REFRAIN:

Myrrh is mine; its bitter perfume   (sung by *Balthazar*)
Breathes a life of gathering gloom;
Sorrowing, sighing, bleeding, dying,
Sealed in the stone-cold tomb.
     REFRAIN:

Glorious now behold Him arise,   (sung by **All**)
King, and God, and Sacrifice;
Heav'n sings Alleluia;
Alleluia the earth replies.
     REFRAIN:

We Wish You a Merry Christmas

Other Title—
A Merry Christmas

Recording Artists—
Phylis Curtin, soprano;
St. Kilian's Boy Choir;
André Kostelanetz and His
Orchestra

Words & Music—
Anonymous sixteenth-
century English folk

Anonymous composers were prone to write lively secular songs just as much as those of a more serious and religious nature. This cheery English carol from the West country of England was probably sung by waits, who were either watchmen or employees of municipalities licensed to perform or sing in parades and other seasonal celebrations, including Christmas, when they caroled in the streets. They probably drank, too, from wassail bowls, some of which could be quite enormous. Such street reveling during the Christmas festivities had its roots in antiquity and the pagan rites of the Winter Solstice.

"We Wish You a Merry Christmas" gives us a good glimpse of sixteenth-century English gaiety, and even today its popular lyrics of good cheer encourage one and all to enjoy the holiday season.

We wish you a Merry Christmas;
We wish you a Merry Christmas;
We wish you a Merry Christmas
And a Happy New Year.
    REFRAIN:
    Good tidings to you wherever you are;
    Good tidings for Christmas
    And a Happy New Year.

Now bring us a figgy pudding;
Now bring us a figgy pudding;
Now bring us a figgy pudding
And a cup of good cheer.
    REFRAIN:

We won't go until we've get some;
We won't go until we've get some;
We won't go until we've get some,
So bring us some here.
    REFRAIN:

We all like our figgy pudding;
We all like our figgy pudding;
We all like our figgy pudding;
With all its good cheer.
    REFRAIN:

We wish you a Merry Christmas;
We wish you a Merry Christmas;
We wish you a Merry Christmas
And a Happy New Year.
    REFRAIN:

Facing page:
As the Old Sing,
the Young Pipe,
Jacob Jordaens (1593–1678),
Alte Pinakothek, Munich

Recording Artists—
The Texas Boys Choir; Gregg Smith Singers; New York Brass and Percussion Ensemble; E. Power Biggs, organ; Gregg Smith, conductor

Words—
William Chatterton Dix (1837–1898), English clergyman and insurance company executive

Music—
Anonymous sixteenth-century English folk

The famous tune "Greensleeves" is the basis for the music of the lovely carol "What Child Is This?" One of the earliest references to it was in 1580, when it was mentioned several times in Shakespeare's comedy play, *The Merry Wives of Windsor*. Strains of the music were also heard in the 1728 satirical ballad opera, *The Beggar's Opera*, by John Gay (1685–1732).

Religiously inspired, William Chatterton Dix wrote his lyrics around 1865 as a six-stanza poem titled *The Manger Throne*. Later he took three of the poem's stanzas and adapted them to the popular sixteenth-century tune of "Greensleeves." In 1871, the text was published in Bramley & Stainer's *Christmas Carols, New and Old*, a highly popular compilation. Because of Dix's efforts, and possibly because the Reverend Henry Ramsden Bramley (1833–1917) may have brought together the tune and the lyrics in the 1871 publication, the legacy of "What Child Is This?" has been sustained over the years by its unforgettable beauty.

The Nativity, Michael Halliday (1822–1869), Stained glass panel from St. Columba Church, Topcliffe, Yorks

What Child is this, who laid to rest,
On Mary's lap is sleeping?
Whom angels greet with anthems sweet
While shepherds watch are keeping?
　　This, this is Christ the King,
　　Whom shepherds guard and angels Sing.
　　Haste, haste to bring Him laud,
　　The Babe, the Son of Mary.

Why lies He in such mean estate
Where ox and ass are feeding?
Good Christians, fear for sinners here,
The silent Word is pleading.
　　Nails, spear shall pierce Him through
　　The cross be borne, for me, for you.
　　Hail, hail the Word made Flesh,
　　The Babe, the Son of Mary.

So bring Him incense, gold and myrrh;
Come peasant king, to own Him.
The King of Kings salvation brings;
Let loving hearts enthrone Him.
　　Raise, raise the song on high,
　　The Virgin sings her lullaby.
　　Joy, joy for Christ is born,
　　The Babe, the Son of Mary.

Other Titles—
*While Shepherds Watched;
While Shepherds Watched
Their Flocks by Night*

Recording Artists—
*Royal Philharmonic
Orchestra & Chorus;
Peter Knight, conductor*

Words—
*Nahum Tate (1652–1715),
English poet laureate*

Music—
*George Frederic Handel
(1685–1759), German-born
English composer*

First published sometime between 1696 and 1700 by Nahum Tate, a Dublin-born Irishman who became Poet Laureate of England, the words of "While Shepherds Watched Their Flocks" are based on paraphrasing of Scriptural text from *St. Luke 2:8–14.* They were written for a tune, at the time over a hundred years old, from the 1592 publication *Whole Book of Psalms* by Thomas Este (c. 1540–1608). This could very well be the oldest Christmas hymn in the form most familiar to us today.

At one time the singing of hymns was considered sacrilegious by some church preachers, particularly the Puritans, who urged their congregations to rely on Biblical *Psalms* for their singing material. Tate's Christmas hymn, however, achieved

The Adoration of the Shepherds, *Rembrandt (1606–1669), The National Gallery, London*

the lofty status of being the only legally authorized hymn by the Church of England, an achievement further consolidated when the hymn was bound up for distribution along with *The Book of Common Prayer*.

Since 1700 a number of variant tunes have been written for "While Shepherds Watched Their Flocks." The first known union of lyrics and music was in the 1861 collection, *Hymns Ancient and Modern*. The music comes from an aria from the 1728 opera *Siroe, King of Persia*, also known as *Cyrus*, by George Frederic Handel. The artistic creation of the great Baroque composer, coupled with Nahum Tate's lyrics, has produced a marvelously appealing Christmas hymn.

> While shepherds watched their flocks by night,
> All seated on the ground,
> The angel of the Lord came down,
> And glory shone around,
> And glory shone around.
>
> "Fear not," he said, for mighty dread
> Had seized their troubled minds.
> "Glad tidings of great joy I bring
> To you and all mankind,
> To you and all mankind."
>
> "To you in David's town this day
> Is born of David's line,
> The Saviour who is Christ the Lord,
> And this shall be the sign,
> And this shall be the sign."
>
> "The heavenly Babe you there shall find
> To human view displayed,
> And meanly wrapped in swathing bands,
> And in a manger laid,
> And in a manger laid."
>
> Thus spake the seraph, and forthwith
> Appeared a shining throng
> Of angels praising God, who thus
> Addressed their joyful song,
> Addressed their joyful song.
>
> "All glory be to God on high,
> And to the earth be peace;
> Goodwill henceforth from heaven to men
> Begin and never cease,
> Begin and never cease!"

Bibliography, Notes, Translators, & Indexes

Bibliography

A — Books

1   *The Batsford Book of Christmas Carols*, Edited by Cyril Taylor; B. T. Batsford, Ltd., London, 1957

2   *Cantate Domino*, Barenreiter, Verlag Kassel, Germany, 1974

3   *Carols and Christmas Music Today*, Hugh Ross; published in *The American Scholar*, Vol.4, No.1, Winter, 1935 Edition

4   *Carols: Their Origin, Music, and Connection with Mystery Plays*, William J. Phillips; Greenwood Press Publishers, Westport, Connecticut, 1921

5   *Carols, The Joy of Christmas*, Edward Heath; Sedgwick & Jackson Ltd., London, 1977

6   *The Christmas Almanack*, Gerard and Patricia Del Re; Doubleday & Company, Inc., Garden City, NY, 1979

7   *Christ and the Carols*, William J. Reynolds; Broadman Press, Nashville, Tennessee, 1967

8   *Christmas and Its Carols*, Reginald Nettel; The Faith Press, London, 1960

9   *Christmas Around the World*, New Orchard Editions Ltd., Robert Rogers House, Copyright 1978 Blanford Press Ltd., 1985 Edition

10   *Christmas Carols: A Reference Guide*, William E. Studwell; Garland Publishing, Inc., New York and London, 1985

11   *Christmas Carols and Their Stories*, Compiled by Christopher Idle; Lion Publishing Corp., Batavia, Illinois, and Sutherland, Australia, 1988

12   *Christmas in Germany*, Josef Ruland; Hohwacht, Bonn, Germany; 1992. Compliments of Goethe House Library New York-German Cultural Center.

13   *Christmas Songs and Their Stories*, Herbert H. Wernecke; The Westminster Press, Philadelphia, 1957

14   *Felix Mendelssohn Bartholdy's Werke*, Vol.XV.6, XV.9, XV.10, Gregg Press, Leipzig, 1967

15   *Gesantansgabe der Musikalischen Werke Von Michael Praetorius*, Arnold Mendelssohn & Willibald Gurlitt, Edited by Frederick Blume; Wolfenbuttel Berlin, 1928–1960

16   *Heritage of Music: Volume 1– Classical Music and Its Origins*, Edited by Michael Raeburn and Alan Kendall; Oxford University Press, New York, 1990

The Adoration of the Magi
*Peter Paul Rubens
(1577–1640), Koninklijke
Museum voor Schone Kunsten,
Antwerp*

17 *The History of Civilization: Part IV, The Age of Faith*, Will Durant; Simon and Schuster, New York, 1950

18 *The History of Civilization: Part VI, The Reformation*, Will Durant; Simon and Schuster, New York, 1957

19 *The Hours of the Divine Office in English and Latin*, The Order of St. Benedict, Inc., Collegeville, Minnesota, 1963

20 *The International Book of Christmas Carols*, Walter Ehret and George Evans; Prentice-Hall, Inc., Englewood Cliffs, New Jersey, 1963

21 *Joel Whitburn's Pop Memories 1890–1954: The History of American Popular Music,* Joel Whitburn; Record Research, Inc., Menomonee Falls, Wisconsin,1986

22 *Moravian Youth Hymnal,* The Interprovincial Board of Christian Education; Moravian Choral in America, Bethlehem, PA, 1942

23 *Musae Sionae, Vols. 2, 6*, Michael Praetorius, 1609; also see *Gesantansgabe der Musikalischen Werke Von Michael Praetorius*

24 *A New Book of Christmas Carols*, Compiled and edited by Ralph Dunstan; Reid Brothers, Ltd., London, 1923

25 *New Catholic Encyclopedia, Volumes 1–14*, The Catholic University of America, Editor-in-Chief, the Most Reverend William J. McDonald, Washington, D.C., 1967

26 *New Catholic Hymnal*, Compiled and edited by Anthony Petti and GeoffreyLaycock; St. Martin's Press, New York, 1971

27 *The New Grove Dictionary of American Music, 4 Vols.*, Edited by H. Wiley Hitchcock and Stanley Sadie; MacMillan Press Limited, London, 1986

28 *The New Grove Dictionary of Music & Musicians, Vols. I-XX*, Edited by Stanley Sadie; MacMillan Publishers Limited, London, 1980

29 *Noëls: A New Collection of Old Carols*, Max and Anne Oberndorfer; H.T. FitzSimons Co., Chicago, 1932

30 *The Orange Carol Book*, Arranged by Mervyn Horder; The Westminster Press, Philadelphia, 1962

31 *The Oxford Book of Carols*, Percy Dearmer, Ralph Vaughan Williams, and Martin Shaw; Oxford University Press, England, 1956. The original text was published in 1928, and another in 1964.

32   *The Oxford Book of Carols*, Edited by Hugh Keyte and Andrew Parrott; Oxford University Press, London and New York, 1994

33   *The Oxford English Dictionary, Vols. I-XII*, The Oxford University Press, Oxford, England, 1933

34   *The Pageantry of Christmas*, Editor, Norman P. Ross; Time Inc. Book Division, 1963

35   *Penguin Book of Carols*, Elizabeth Poston; Harmondsworth, England, 1965

36   *Piae Cantiones*, Edited by Timo Makinen; Karkkilan Kirjapaino, Helsinski, Finland, 1968. This is a reprint of the original 1582 text.

37   *Publishing Glad Tidings: Essays on Christmas Music*, William E. Studwell and Dorothy E. Jones; The Haworth Press, Inc., New York and London, 1998

38   *The Reader's Digest Merry Christmas Songbook*, Edited by William L. Simon; The Reader's Digest Association, Inc., Pleasantville, New York, 1981

39   *Silent Night, Holy Night: The Immortal Song and its Origin*, Michael Gundringer; Lamprechtshausen, Salzburg, c.1950

40   *Silent Night, Holy Night: The Story of a Lovely Christmas Song*, The Frederick H. Jaenicken Company, Chicago, Illinois, 1935

41   *Songs of the Nativity: Being Christmas Carols, Ancient and Modern*, Edited by William H. Husk; John Camden Hotten, Piccadilly, London, c.1884

42   *The Summit Choir Book*, The Dominican Nuns of Summit, New Jersey, Monastery of Our Lady of the Rosary, 1983

43   *Today's Missal: Advent/Ordinary Time*, Edited by Bari Colomari; Oregon Press, Portland, Oregon, 1994

44   *Translations and Annotations of Choral Repertoire, Sacred Latin Texts*, Edited and annotated by Ron Jeffers; Earthsongs, Corvallis, Oregon, 1988

45   *Twelve Days of Christmas: A Celebration and History,* Leigh Grant; Harry N. Abrams, Inc., New York, 1995

B — Audio Recording Jackets, Inserts, & Booklets

1   *Christmas in the New World*, The Western Wind Singers, The Musical Heritage Society/ MHS 4077, 1979; notes by Lawrence Bennett

2   *Noël: The Mormon Tabernacle Choir—A Worldwide Christmas Celebration*, Bonneville Classics, Salt Lake City, Utah, 1993

3   *This is Christmas*; The Mormon Tabernacle Choir, Bonneville Classics, Salt Lake City, Utah, 1994

C — Other Sources

1   Newspaper article titled "Fa La La! 'Tis the Season to Be Warmed by the Undying Music of Christmas Past and Present," Connie Lauerman, *The Chicago Tribune Magazine*, December 23, 1990

2   Information provided by Louise Panczner from her church publication *The Weekly Bridge*, January 1, 1992

3   Newspaper article titled "Christmas Carols Have Surprising Origins," Associated Press, *The Atlantic City Press*, December 12, 1994

4   "Christmas Carol Has Special Meaning" pamphlet provided by Mr. Don Goodman of Allentown, PA, and pastor Boyd Fox of the Haddon Heights Methodist Church, December, 1996

5   *Hymn Notes Christmas 2003* by Donna Wessel Walker, St. Andrew's Episcopal Church, Ann Arbor, MI

Notes

To understand Keys to Notes, please refer to the Bibliography, pages 93–96.

A numbers refer to Books

B numbers refer to Audio Recording Jackets, Inserts, and Booklets

C numbers refer to Other Sources

The Historical Perspective

A1, p.11

A3, p.19

A4, pp.13–19

A7, p.18

A8, pp.46-48

A16, pp.34-38

A17, p.635

A18, pp.778-779

A20

A25, vol. 3, pp.130–132, 655-659

A31, pp.v-vi

A35, p.211

B1

Carols

1	Adeste Fideles	A13, 20, 26, 30, 32, 38 B3
2	Angels from the Realms of Glory	A6, 11, 20, 38
3	Away in a Manger	A10, 13, 26, 27, 32, 43
4	Cantique de Noël	A10, 20, 28
5	Deck the Halls with Boughs of Holly	A6, 10, 20, 38 B3
6	Es ist ein' Ros' entsprungen	A13, 15, 20, 22, 30, 31, 35, 43 B2
7	The First Nowell	A10, 20, 32, 38
8	God Rest Ye Merry, Gentlemen	A10, 20, 38
9	Good Christian Men, Rejoice	A10, 20, 32, 36, 43
10	Good King Wenceslas	A9, 10, 20, 30, 36, 37
11	Hark! The Herald Angels Sing	A6, 14, 20, 25, 31 C1 D5
12	The Holly and the Ivy	A9, 10, 20, 24, 32, 34
13	It Came Upon the Midnight Clear	A6, 10, 11, 20 C1
14	Joy to the World	A10, 13, 20, 32, 43
15	Les Anges dans nos campagnes	A10, 32, 38, 43 B3
16	O Little Town of Bethlehem	A6, 10, 20 D5
17	O Tannenbaum	A9, 10, 20, 32, 34
18	Stille Nacht, heilige Nacht	A10, 12, 20, 21, 28, 30, 39, 40 C1
19	The Twelve Days of Christmas	A38, 41, 45 C4
20	Veni, Emmanuel	A2, 13, 19, 20, 21, 26, 37, 42, 44
21	Wassail Song	A5, 10, 20, 31, 32, 33
22	We Three Kings of Orient Are	A6, 20, 28, 43 C1, 2
23	We Wish You a Merry Christmas	A10, 33, 38
24	What Child Is This?	A6, 20, 28, 37, 38
25	While Shepherds Watched Their Flocks	A10, 32, 38, 43 C1, 3

The Flight into Egypt,
c.1850–1853,
Alexander-Gabriele Decamps
(1803–1860),
Brooklyn Museum

✹ *Translators*

Adeste Fideles—Rev. Francis Oakeley (1802–1880)

Cantique de Noël—John Sullivan Dwight (1818–1893)

Es ist ein' Ros' entsprungen—Theodore Baker (1851–1934)
                                          —Harriet R. K. Spaeth (1845–1925)

Les Anges dans nos campagnes—James Chadwick (1813–1882)

O Tannenbaum—George K. Evans (b.1917)

Stille Nacht, heilige Nacht—John Freeman Young (1820–1885)

Veni, Emmanuel—John Mason Neale (1818–1866)

Title Index

Audio Index

Title	Performed By
Adeste Fideles *(O Come All Ye Faithful)*	Vienna Boys Choir & The London Symphony Orchestra ℗ 1989 SONY BMG MUSIC ENTERTAINMENT Courtesy of Iliad, Inc.
Angels from the Realms of Glory	The Ambrosian Singers; John McCarthy, conductor; Leon Goossens, oboe; Marie Goossens, harp; with organ and chimes Courtesy of Reader's Digest Music
Away in a Manger	Royal Philharmonic Orchestra & Chorus; Peter Knight, conductor Courtesy of Ardee Music Publishing, Inc.
Cantique de Noël *(O Holy Night)*	RCA Victor Singers; Richard Westenburg, conductor ℗ 1993 BMG Entertainment
Deck the Halls with Boughs of Holly	Norman Luboff Choir Originally released 1952 SONY BMG MUSIC ENTERTAINMENT
Es ist ein' Ros' entsprungen *(Lo, How a Rose E'er Blooming)*	The DePaur Chorus; Leonard DePaur, conductor Originally released 1955 SONY BMG MUSIC ENTERTAINMENT
The First Nowell *(The First Noël)*	Vienna Boys Choir & The London Symphony Orchestra ℗ 1993 SONY BMG MUSIC ENTERTAINMENT Courtesy of Iliad, Inc.
God Rest Ye Merry, Gentlemen	RCA Victor Singers; Richard Westenburg, conductor ℗ 1993 BMG Entertainment
Good Christian Men, Rejoice	Royal Philharmonic Orchestra & Chorus; Peter Knight, conductor Courtesy of Ardee Music Publishing, Inc.
Good King Wenceslas	Vienna Boys Choir & The London Symphony Orchestra ℗ 1994 SONY BMG MUSIC ENTERTAINMENT Courtesy of Iliad, Inc.

Hark! The Herald Angels Sing	Mormon Tabernacle Choir; Richard P. Condie, director; Alexander Schreiner & Frank Asper, organ Originally released 1960 SONY BMG MUSIC ENTERTAINMENT
The Holly and the Ivy	The Texas Boys Choir; Gregg Smith Singers; New York Brass and Percussion Ensemble; E. Power Biggs, organ; Gregg Smith, conductor Originally released 1968 SONY BMG MUSIC ENTERTAINMENT
It Came Upon the Midnight Clear	Mormon Tabernacle Choir; Richard P. Condie, director Originally released 1961 SONY BMG MUSIC ENTERTAINMENT
Joy to the World	Royal Philharmonic Orchestra & Chorus; Peter Knight, conductor Courtesy of Ardee Music Publishing, Inc.
Les Anges dans nos campagnes *(Angels We Have Heard on High)*	Vienna Boys Choir & The London Symphony Orchestra ℗ 1993 SONY BMG MUSIC ENTERTAINMENT Courtesy of Iliad, Inc.
O Little Town of Bethlehem	RCA Victor Singers; Richard Westenburg, conductor ℗ 1993 BMG Entertainment
O Tannenbaum	Marilyn Horne, mezzo-soprano; Mormon Tabernacle Choir; Columbia Symphony Orchestra; Jerold Ottley, conductor ℗ 1983 SONY BMG MUSIC ENTERTAINMENT
Stille Nacht, heilige Nacht *(Silent Night)*	Mormon Tabernacle Choir; Alexander Schreiner & Frank Asper, organ Originally released 1959 SONY BMG MUSIC ENTERTAINMENT
The Twelve Days of Christmas	Mormon Tabernacle Choir; Richard P. Condie, director; New York Philharmonic Orchestra; Leonard Bernstein, conductor Originally released 1963 SONY BMG MUSIC ENTERTAINMENT

Veni, Emmanuel *(O Come, O Come Emmanuel)*	RCA Victor Singers; Richard Westenburg, conductor ℗ 1993 BMG Entertainment
Wassail Song *(Here We Come A-Caroling)*	Mormon Tabernacle Choir; Richard P. Condie, director Originally released 1961 SONY BMG MUSIC ENTERTAINMENT
We Three Kings of Orient Are	RCA Victor Singers; Richard Westenburg, conductor ℗ 1993 BMG Entertainment
We Wish You a Merry Christmas	Phylis Curtin, soprano; St. Kilian's Boy Choir; André Kostelanetz and His Orchestra Originally released 1965 SONY BMG MUSIC ENTERTAINMENT
What Child Is This?	The Texas Boys Choir; Gregg Smith Singers; New York Brass and Percussion Ensemble; E. Power Biggs, organ; Gregg Smith, conductor Originally released 1965 SONY BMG MUSIC ENTERTAINMENT
While Shepherds Watched Their Flocks	Royal Philharmonic Orchestra & Chorus; Peter Knight, conductor Courtesy of Reader's Digest Music

Also from Ron Clancy

The Millennia Collection:
Glorious Christmas Music, Songs and Carols

American Christmas Classics

Children's Christmas Classics

PLANNED VOLUMES IN THE SERIES

Christmas Carols from the British Isles

Worldwide Christmas Classics

Sacred Christmas Music

French Noëls & Music

German Christmas Music

Golden Musical Ornaments

About the Author

Ronald M. Clancy, born in 1944, is married and a graduate of George Washington University, where he earned a B.A. degree in Journalism. His interest in Christmas music began as a youth in an orphanage in Philadelphia, where he sang in the boys choir. In 1982 he began to assemble a sizable Christmas music library. By 1989 his continued interest in Christmas music led him on his journey to compile and author the landmark *THE MILLENNIA COLLECTION: Glorious Christmas Music, Songs and Carols*, a series of ten distinct Christmas music products planned for future launch.